"*Discovering Your Leader* ...ten. The contents are stunni... ...ed it firsthand. I have seen the p... ...ough its contents. If you wish to understand yoursell, ...d the future of the church, absorb the contents of this remarkable book."

Michael O. Emerson, professor of sociology, Rice University, and author of *Divided by Faith*

"The starting point for every person, leader, coach, parent, church or business seeking to make an impact is to ask two questions—who has God wired me to be *and* what has God gifted me to do. Drawing from thirty years of coaching leaders (including me!), Dave Olson has put together the most helpful tool for discovering how to lead with your strengths. This book should be read by *every* leader. Not only will they be more effective, they will also have a lot more fun!"

Ray Johnston, pastor, Bayside Church, Sacramento

"David Olson has given the church and its leaders a gift. With a method that is easily understandable and yet quite profound, leaders are given new lenses to understand their ministry style. These new perspectives not only enable leaders to better serve the church but also to take concrete steps, in concert with the Spirit, to refine their ministry stance. I highly recommend this book for leaders and leadership teams. The insights gained and acted on will further the work of Christ in the world."

Kurt Fredrickson, associate dean, Fuller Theological Seminary

"Leadership matters, and as such, there are many books on leadership, but what makes this book stand apart is both its simplicity and profundity. By focusing on the three core elements of spirituality, chemistry and strategy, this book doesn't just detail what leadership is, but rather helps its readers engage in an important journey of examination and introspection of one's leadership style. This book is a gift to leaders and to the larger church."

Eugene Cho, pastor, Quest Church, Seattle, and author of *Overrated*

"In an age where style is too often championed over substance, Dave Olson is one of a few proven leaders who can be trusted time and again for credible insight and experiential wisdom. In *Discovering Your Leadership Style*, he delivers the fundamental goods of effective leadership beyond pithy statements, favorited tweets and untested boasts. Biblically sound, practical and engaging, this book will help you (and your team) get beyond mere talent to Christ-centered competency as you lead others for him."

Mark DeYmaz, pastor, Mosaic Church of Central Arkansas

"*Discovering Your Leadership Style* is one of the most helpful books on leadership that I have come across. Using a new and innovative model, Dave provides Christian leaders with a practical and easy-to-use method for developing into better and stronger leaders, as well as helping their staff and lay leaders do the same. I highly recommend this book."

Todd Wilson, CEO, Exponential Conference

"I have had the honor of serving alongside Dave Olson for many years through Covenant Church Planting. Dave's concepts help individuals and teams to discover their unique balance of spirituality, chemistry and strategy and to launch personal and ministry growth. His leadership theories and applications will bear much fruit for all who delve into this book!"

John Teter, church planting team leader, Evangelical Covenant Church

"As the leader of a college, I have been seeking a tool to help us identify exactly what *Discovering Your Leadership Style* has identified—how best to understand and use our leadership gifting and styles. This book is the catalyst for us to meet as staff and faculty to strengthen and deepen our team by understanding how each of us is gifted by God to lead. This new book will be helpful to every leader who works in parachurch ministries."

Keith Hamilton, president, Alaska Christian College

"Dave Olson has been a mentor, friend, and more broadly an activist for healthy Christian leadership. His insights have been a blessing to me and through this book, he will be a blessing to many, many more. For those with a desire to increase your leadership influence and skills, this is a must read."

Efrem Smith, President and CEO of World Impact Incorporated

DAVID T. OLSON

DISCOVERING YOUR LEADERSHIP STYLE

THE POWER OF CHEMISTRY, STRATEGY AND SPIRITUALITY

IVP Books

An imprint of InterVarsity Press
Downers Grove, Illinois

InterVarsity Press
P.O. Box 1400, Downers Grove, IL 60515-1426
World Wide Web: www.ivpress.com
Email: email@ivpress.com

InterVarsity Press® is the book-publishing division of InterVarsity Christian Fellowship/USA®, a movement
of students and faculty active on campus at hundreds of universities, colleges and schools of nursing in the
United States of America, and a member movement of the International Fellowship of Evangelical Students.
For information about local and regional activities, write Public Relations Dept., InterVarsity Christian
Fellowship/USA, 6400 Schroeder Rd., P.O. Box 7895, Madison, WI 53707-7895, or visit the IVCF website at
www.intervarsity.org.

While all stories in this book are true, some names and identifying information in this book have been
changed to protect the privacy of the individuals involved.

Cover design: Cindy Kiple
Interior design: Beth Hagenberg
Images: © johnbloor/iStockphoto

ISBN 978-0-8308-4113-4 (print)
ISBN 978-0-8308-9591-5 (digital)

Printed in the United States of America

green press INITIATIVE InterVarsity Press is committed to protecting the environment and to the responsible use of
natural resources. As a member of Green Press Initiative we use recycled paper whenever
possible. To learn more about the Green Press Initiative, visit www.greenpressinitiative.org.

Library of Congress Cataloging-in-Publication Data
A catalog record for this book is available from the Library of Congress.

P	18	17	16	15	14	13	12	11	10	9	8	7	6	5	4	3	2	1
Y	29	28	27	26	25	24	23	22	21	20	19	18	17	16	15	14

Contents

THE MODEL

Section One provides a comprehensive introduction to the leadership stool model. It shows how spirituality, chemistry and strategy flow out of the Great Commandment and the Great Commission. This model is in harmony with how God created our hearts, souls, minds and strength. It defines what makes leadership Christian. This section links the model to how God has given all Christians gifts, passions and personalities with which to serve him. It marks the beginning of the adventure of an increased self understanding and a deeper realization of what it means to be a Christian leader.

1

A New Leadership Model

> *It was the best of times, it was the worst of times,*
> *it was the age of wisdom, it was the age of foolishness,*
> *it was the epoch of belief, it was the epoch of incredulity,*
> *it was the season of Light, it was the season of Darkness,*
> *it was the spring of hope, it was the winter of despair.*
>
> **Charles Dickens**

The first line from Dickens's great novel not only describes life in England and France 250 years ago but also describes the religious landscape of America today. It is the best of times and the worst of times. It is an era of great opportunities and relentless challenges. The American church is in crisis, and Christian leaders must face this crisis head-on. It is much more challenging to lead a church or Christian organization today than it was just twenty years ago. How can we learn to lead wisely in an increasingly post-Christian, postmodern and multiethnic world?

The place to begin is for each of us to personalize leadership's foundational questions:

- Am I really a leader?
- How do I know if God has given me the gifts and abilities needed to lead people?
- How can I grow in leadership?
- Does God give every Christian the potential to lead?
- What makes Christian leadership different from secular leadership?

These questions give voice to our soul's longing to be used by God, while recognizing the insecurity we often feel when evaluating our own leadership abilities. Four additional questions can help frame this challenge:

♦ Are people born with innate leadership gifts—Is it nature?

♦ Can leadership improve with experience and effort—Is it nurture?

♦ Is Christian leadership primarily about organizational strategy, as some Christian leadership books imply?

♦ Or is Christian leadership primarily about deep spirituality, as others imply?

The goal of this book is to present a simple yet robust model for Christian leadership. I believe this model will give you clarity as to how God has created you and how you can become the leader God intended you to be. The boundaries of your imagination will be stretched. You will gain a deep appreciation of your unique gifts. You will find a new frame of reference for understanding how to lead in a challenging culture with wisdom, grace, love and strength.

Let us begin with this observation: *Leadership strength is the slowest growing quality in the life of a Christian leader.* What a sad reality! Someone once defined leadership as "the ability to hide your panic from others." We all wish it was an easy course to master. Unfortunately, it is definitely a graduate-level program. Every other competency in Christian ministry is easier to develop. What makes leadership so difficult and daunting is that it encompasses how you respond to each ministry situation you face.

Here is a second observation: *The younger leaders are, the stronger they believe themselves to be; the more experience leaders gain, the more they become aware of how much more they need to learn.* When I talk to young or inexperienced leaders who hold an unrealistically high opinion of their own leadership ability, I remind them that if they are really that good, they have already maximized their full leadership potential. The only direction for them to go is downward!

Many people look to personality assessments to gain clarity and self-understanding about how to lead—instruments like the Myers-Briggs Type Indicator (MBTI), StrengthsFinder, the DISC Personal Profile and a host of other assessments. These tools can help leaders to understand their personality and identify certain qualities of leadership. I love them all for the self-understanding they provide. However, they are not designed to help leaders discover what type of leader they are, or how they are meant to lead, or how to grow as a leader.

It is even more difficult to find tools that will help a Christian leader learn to lead as Jesus led. Books written to describe the essence of Christian leadership abound, and many are excellent. But it is challenging to find a biblical model that provides immediate clarity and focus regarding how to lead well in the rough and tumble world of a church or Christian organization. Wouldn't it be wonderful if there was a model that was simple, clear and usable with people on all levels of leadership?

MY EXPERIENCE IN LEADERSHIP DEVELOPMENT

My introduction into a focused quest to understand leadership development began twenty-two years ago when I was asked by a Christian organization to help them adapt a new and innovative model for evaluating the potential of young Christian leaders for a specific role—starting new churches. For the last twenty years, I have led eighty assessment centers that have taken almost a thousand young, gifted Christian leaders (along with their spouses) on an intensive four-day leadership evaluation process to discover if they have the character, calling, gifts, passions, habits and entrepreneurial ability to start a new church.

Each center is composed of twelve to fifteen candidates who have passed a pre-assessment screening and have submitted multiple references verifying their past ministry experience and fruitfulness. A trained assessor team of twelve to fifteen people get to know each person in depth through test results, sermon presentations, small-group simulations, interviews, group problem-solving activities and ministry skill evaluations. In addition, a professional counselor helps the candidates and spouses discern deeper issues that may short-circuit healthy ministry.

Over the four-day period, a comprehensive picture of each candidate begins to emerge. During the rigorous schedule of twelve-plus hours a day, some participants rise in our estimation while others decline. We may discover sterling character or uncover dubious behavior. We meet candidates with accurate self-understanding and others with delusional self-perceptions.

While our Assessment Center looks at twenty-two different ministry factors, the following questions rise above the rest and can be complex to assess:

- Is this person a leader?

- Do others follow him or her?

- Have the individual's leadership abilities been formed by Scripture, fruitful experience and the work of the Holy Spirit?

- Does this person have potential flaws that could harm the ministry and devastate the people who follow him or her?

These questions and experiences have ignited in me a deep desire to develop a Christian leadership model that can build up the kingdom of God by forming Christ-centered, healthy, missional leaders.

THE LEADERSHIP STOOL

This book will look at Christian leadership through a new paradigm, using the visual of a three-legged stool. The Leadership Stool model was developed to help leaders and churches understand how three factors—*spirituality*, *chemistry* and *strategy*—work together to produce fruitful Christian leaders that further the work of God in the life of a church or organization.

The Leadership Stool model is simple. You will fill out an online inventory that takes five minutes to complete and immediately receive the resulting report. It takes just a few minutes to understand the core model. The three legs of spirituality, chemistry and strategy are easy to remember, straightforward and practical. Simple is good! As Winston Churchill said, "All the greatest things are simple, and many can be expressed in a single word: Freedom; Justice; Honour; Duty; Mercy; Hope."[1]

But this model is also deep. It is designed to help Christian leaders grow deeper, wiser, stronger and more influential in their leadership. It is designed to immerse leaders into deeper levels of insight, bringing them to a clear realization of how God has created them to lead and how they can grow stronger as leaders.

Here is the description of the three legs:

♦ *Spirituality* encompasses all that it means to love God.

♦ *Chemistry* encompasses all that it means to love people.

♦ *Strategy* encompasses all that it means to love the world by fulfilling the mission of God in the world.

This model is based on how Jesus taught, led and ministered, and on how he trained his disciples to lead and minister. Spirituality is shown to us in the relationship Jesus had with his Father. Chemistry is shown to us in the relationships Jesus had with his disciples and the people he met in the towns and villages. Strategy is shown to us in the mission Jesus had toward the world, especially toward the lost and the hurting.

This model will strengthen your twelve core leadership foundations (discussed in section 2) and provide you with tools to coach and mentor other leaders. It will help you strengthen your team dynamics. It will also become a paradigm for understanding your church or organization, explaining many of the complex and confusing problems that occur in its structure. It will encourage you to go deep into your own personhood to let God shape you as a Christian leader. Most important, you will discover your specific Christian leadership style so that you can lead in a manner that focuses and develops the unique gifts, passions and personality God has created in you.

Your leadership potential for Christ will be determined by how well you develop the legs of spirituality, chemistry and strategy in your life. The best leaders seek to grow in all three legs, causing their leadership to become stronger and more balanced. This threefold focus will ensure that spiritual depth (spirituality), relational health (chemistry) and ministry fruitfulness (strategy) are authentically lived out through your life and ministry. Then you can lead like Jesus, by ministering courageously and fruitfully in the realms of the mind (strategy), the soul (chemistry) and the heart (spirituality).

Yet three strong legs do not automatically produce a good leader. A three-legged stool needs its seat to unify the legs so that the stool can become useful. The seat of the Leadership Stool is *leadership wisdom*. Building on the strong foundation of increased spirituality, chemistry and strategy, growth in leadership wisdom will move you to a new level of leadership capacity and capability.

HOW TO GET THE MOST OUT OF THIS BOOK

This book is designed to be experiential. At the end of each chapter you will find an action-oriented mission assignment that will let you immediately integrate and implement what you learned in the chapter. The first assignment takes you to the Leadership Stool Inventory, which is available online at no charge. After completing the multiple-choice questionnaire, click "Submit," and your leadership profile will display on your screen.

The end of each section contains an online activity to help individual leaders, teams, churches and organizations put the ideas in this book into practice. At the end of this section, your staff or board can use the online "Team Profile Tool." The online activity at the end of the second section focuses on developing your personal leadership strength. Mentoring and coaching other leaders is the theme of the third online activity. The fourth online activity can be used to help select both lay leaders and staff. The final online activity in the fifth section is titled "A Passion to

Figure 1.1. Leadership stool

Serve," a gift assessment tool for your whole congregation.

This book will help you understand how God has formed you, how to lead using your unique style, how to grow stronger in the core foundations of leadership, how to become a better team leader and how to mobilize your whole church or organization to use their giftedness to serve Christ.

Are you ready to discover your Christian leadership style?

MISSION ASSIGNMENT—TAKE THE LEADERSHIP STOOL INVENTORY

Begin your journey by taking the Leadership Stool Inventory, which will help you to assess your leadership ability and understand your leadership style.

If you are a senior pastor, go to www.sixstyles.org/seniorpastor.php.

If you are a pastor on a church staff, go to www.sixstyles.org/staff.php.

If you are a youth pastor, go to www.sixstyles.org/youthpastor.php.

If you are a lay leader in a church, go to www.sixstyles.org/layleader.php.

If you are in leadership at a Christian organization, go to www.sixstyles.org/Christianleader.php.

If you are on the ministry staff of a Christian organization, go to www.sixstyles.org/ministrystaff.php.

If you are in an administrative support role at a church or Christian organization, go to www.sixstyles.org/administrativesupport.php.

If you are a ministry spouse, go to www.sixstyles.org/ministryspouse.php.

2

Simple, Yet Deep

Leadership . . . defies definition. No combination of talents can guarantee it. No process of training can create it where the spark does not exist. The qualities of leadership are universal. They are found in the poor and the rich, the humble and the proud, the common man, and the brilliant thinker; they are qualities that suggest paradox rather than pattern. But wherever they are found, leadership makes things happen.

Carole Kismaric and Charles Mikolayca

A new book on Christian leadership by Albert Mohler, *The Conviction to Lead*,[1] describes twenty-five qualities that a Christian leader should develop. All are helpful, but developing skill in twenty-five separate leadership areas seems overwhelming. In an online resource, business leader Mark Cuban and other members of *Shark Tank* share "50 Qualities of a Successful Leader."[2] Here are the fifty:

Uniqueness	Focus	Personal Motivation	Clarity	Capacity
Passion	Relevance	Innovative	Excellence	Solutions
Wisdom	Production	Response	Genuineness	Communication
Authenticity	Character	Value	Profit	Knowledge
Options	Priorities	Sacrifice	Investment	Partnerships
Goals	Viability	Sustainability	Results	Multi-Generational
Modeling	Preparation	Vision	Simple	Right Fit
In Demand	Teachability	Intelligence	The Ability To Say No	Financial Viability
Expertise	Distinctiveness	Learned	Opportunistic	Faithful
Perspective	Chemistry	Competence	Joy	Negotiating Skills

Again, all are valuable, but *fifty*?

A SIMPLE LEADERSHIP MODEL

This book focuses instead on a simple yet deep model. Simple is good, but if a model lacks depth, it will create little ability to bring about life transformation in yourself and others. The process of unpacking the depth of this simple model begins with the following question: "What are the most important instructions of Jesus to his followers?" While there are many possible answers, most Christian scholars agree the two most important utterances of Jesus are the Great Commandment and the Great Commission. In Mark 12, Jesus was asked which commandment was the greatest:

"The most important one," answered Jesus, "is this: 'Hear, O Israel: The Lord our God, the Lord is one. Love the Lord your God with all your heart and with all your soul and with all your mind and with all your strength.' The second is this: 'Love your neighbor as yourself.' There is no commandment greater than these." (Mk 12:29-31)

The Great Commission, Jesus' last instructions to his disciples, is found in the last two verses of Matthew:

Therefore go and make disciples of all nations, baptizing them in the name of the Father and of the Son and of the Holy Spirit, and teaching them to obey everything I have commanded you. (Mt 28:19-20)

These two Scriptures are the foundations of the Leadership Stool model. The three legs of the stool are the three primary foundations of Christian leadership: spirituality, chemistry and strategy. Spirituality focuses on loving God with all your heart ("Love the Lord your God with all your heart"). Chemistry focuses on loving people with all your soul ("Love your neighbor as yourself"). Strategy focuses on loving the mission of God with all your mind ("Go and make disciples of all nations").

Where do a person's abilities in spirituality, chemistry and strategy come from? The answer is in the way God formed each of our hearts, souls and minds. Based on how you were created and gifted by God, you are naturally strongest in one of these three areas and develop a preference for using your heart, soul or mind as the primary way to give and receive meaning in your life. Every Christian is best at one of the three legs and not as strong in the other two.

One of my favorite devotional books is *Celtic Daily Prayer*. It is Christocentric and uses ancient texts that remain relevant today to give voice to our faith. Most mornings for the last ten years, as part of my spiritual disciplines I wake up and begin my day by saying aloud the Morning Prayer, which includes this call and response:

Who is it that you seek?
We seek the Lord our God.
Do you seek Him with all your heart?
Amen. Lord, have mercy.
Do you seek Him with all your soul?
Amen. Lord, have mercy.
Do you seek Him with all your mind?
Amen. Lord, have mercy.
Do you seek Him with all your strength?
Amen. Christ, have mercy.[3]

A few years ago my wife, Shelly, and I had the privilege of crafting a "Missional Monastic Tour" through England with some friends of ours. In the middle of our tour, we stayed for four days at the Christian community that birthed *Celtic Daily Prayer*, the Northumbria Community. Before breakfast, lunch, dinner and bedtime, we interrupted our day to join together in prayer and worship. We gathered in a small, primitive hand-sawn chapel for Morning Prayer, Midday Prayer, Evening Prayer and Compline. It was such a wonderful lesson in giving God first place in our hearts and lives.

We came to the Northumbria Community to "Love the Lord our God with all our heart, soul, mind and strength." This foundational verse helps us understand how we are to live our life before God, and it is essential to keep this central as we explore our leadership styles.

FOUNDATIONS OF CHRISTIAN LEADERSHIP

Spirituality. How do we love God with all our *heart?* Jesus used the word *heart,* which in the Greek New Testament is the word *kardia,* to describe the part of each human that is meant to connect with God himself. It is with our hearts that we express our appreciation, longing, dependence and affection for God. *Spirituality* is the word we will use to describe this relationship with God.

Spirituality finds its fulfillment in understanding the essence and experiencing the depth of the true God. Spirituality is the basis for our connection with God and the experience of communion with God. For Christians, spirituality is a gift from God that changes us through the work of grace. Spirituality is what God uses to recreate us into true humans as we experience God's love, grace and holiness.

Spirituality is highly linked to artistic instincts and ability, combined with a desire to create, whether in music, art, writing or craftsmanship. People who are strongest in spirituality often have an appreciation for the symbolic or ritual. They have a deep need to express, in some physical way, what they intuitively understand in their heart. They are drawn to outward symbols that portray what they experience deep within their inner being but find difficult to express with words alone.

Chemistry. The second part of the Great Commandment ("Love your neighbor as yourself") instructs us to love people with all our *soul.* The Greek word for soul is *psyche*—the inner part of our being that allows us to connect emotionally with other people. It is with our soul that we create the love connection with those around us. *Chemistry* is the word we will use to describe this relational engagement.

Chemistry finds its greatest joy in human interaction. This amazing gift is used to help us know each other, engage with each other and love each other. Those strongest in chemistry are people-centered and feel that they would "die" if they were left alone. They love all forms of human interaction and bring a zest to life that is infectious. Chemistry people can be unusually good at displaying the fruits of the Spirit.

Strategy. The Great Commission teaches us to love the world with all our *mind*. The most common Greek word that is translated "mind" in the New Testament is the word *nous*. Our mind refers to the part of our brain that allows us to think in an orderly manner so that we can accomplish real physical progress in our world. *Strategy* is the word we will use to describe how we love the world.

The strategy gift creates the desire to turn dreams and ideas into reality. Strategy people want to make a physical difference in this world. They spend much of their time thinking about the future and try to create a sequential process that will make the future better. Strategy people get frustrated when others just talk about what they want to do but never get it done. Strategy should produce action! This gift works itself out in plans, procedures, physical structures, stream-lined organizations and actual progress.

Leadership wisdom. Finally, we are to love and lead as Jesus loved and led, using all of our *strength*. This fourth word refers to the role of the seat in the Leadership Stool model. Our calling as a Christian leader is to develop strength through the use of leadership wisdom. Wisdom is a predominant biblical theme throughout both the Old and New Testaments and should be a primary quality of every Christian leader. Leadership wisdom brings an equilibrium to a church or organization by making sure the three legs are valued, held together and acted out in balance.

Strength is a fitting descriptor of the hard work necessary to become a wise and godly leader. Everyone who has lived in the leadership arena knows that strength is leadership's daily requirement. *Leadership wisdom* is the phrase we will use to describe this attribute.

These four simple words: *heart*, *soul*, *mind* and *strength*, will bring you into the very core of God's plan for you, to learn what it means to love and lead with spirituality, chemistry, strategy and leadership wisdom.

The rest of this book will provide you with a complete description of the Leadership Stool model. As you read on, you will discover that the more you understand the model, the more useful this tool will become in the development of your leadership potential.

MISSION ASSIGNMENT—UNDERSTANDING YOUR REPORT

Your Leadership Stool report displays four percentages that reflect your strength in spirituality, chemistry, strategy and leadership wisdom. Each score is determined by the combination of your gifts, passions, personality, habits, experience, motivation, work ethic, standards and responsiveness to God's voice in your life. Your score is unique to you. The significance of each percentage is to provide you with a quantitative measure that reflects how God designed you, your relative strength in these four areas and how you have developed habits that enhance each area. Knowing your score and what each percentage means is the first step in the journey of becoming a better, wiser, stronger and more fruitful Christian leader.

KEY OBSERVATIONS

The bar graph on the first page of your report shows your strength in spirituality, chemistry and strategy. Accompanying each bar is a percentage that reflects how you rated yourself in each area.

The highest bar is your strongest leg and is your God-given gift. Most of your ministry fruit will come from this leg.

The second highest bar is your intermediate leg. Strengthening your intermediate leg is the easiest way to become a stronger leader.

The lowest bar is your weakest leg. If left undeveloped, this will negatively affect your potential as a leader.

On page three of the report is a green bar that shows how you scored in leadership wisdom. This scale evaluates how you develop other leaders and measures your leadership fruitfulness, instincts and habits.

The average score received by those who have taken the Leadership Stool Inventory in each of the four scales is 55 percent.

SPECIFIC PATTERNS

You qualify as a *balanced leader* if all of your scores in the first chart are above the sixtieth percentile and the percentage difference between your strongest and your weakest leg is 20 percent or less. Balanced leaders are able to use multiple leadership styles, determined by the situation in which they find themselves.

When your highest score in the first chart is over the seventy-fifth percentile and your lowest score is under the fiftieth percentile, you are what is called a *focused leader.* This means you use your Christian leadership style in almost all situations you face. Learning how to sharpen the focus of leading with your particular style can help you become strong at leading through your best gifts. Focused leaders can become stronger leaders by identifying and recruiting a team of people who possess complementary styles to their own.

Chapter 22 contains more information on balanced versus focused leaders.

A score higher than the sixty-fifth percentile in the second (green) graph (your leadership wisdom score) indicates that you have a strong understanding of many of the functions of the leadership role.

Your Christian leadership style is identified on the second page of your report. Learning about your style and how to use it as a leader is the most important outcome of reading this book. The third section of this book is devoted to helping you learn how to use your particular leadership style.

If your spirituality score is below the fortieth percentile, you need to make significant improvements in the three core foundations of spirituality so that you may grow deeper in Christ. For a Christian leader, taking care of your spiritual life must always be a priority.

If all of your scores are under the thirtieth percentile, this may mean that you should carefully consider whether this is the right time to serve in a leadership capacity. It is best to first strengthen yourself in at least two legs of the Leadership Stool model.

3

What Makes
Leadership Christian?

The most precious and intangible quality of leadership is trust: the confidence that the one who leads will act in the best interest of those who follow. . . . Leadership's imperative is a "sense of rightness," knowing when to advance and when to pause, when to criticize and when to praise, how to encourage others to excel. . . . Integrity recognizes external obligation, but it heeds the quiet voice within, rather than the clamor without.

Carole Kismaric and Charles Mikolaycak

I hope this chapter will challenge your leadership assumptions. Why? Most Christian leaders are so influenced by the thought patterns of secular leadership that they cannot hear the new and radical message of Jesus regarding Christian leadership.

This chapter will lay out two foundational principles of leadership for a follower of Jesus and two preconditions of leading as Jesus led. I hope it will debunk some of the false understandings of leadership that we have acquired from our culture.

TWO PRINCIPLES OF CHRISTIAN LEADERSHIP
This is the first principle:

Christian leadership occurs when a person influences other people to move forward in fulfilling God's will for their lives, their families, their churches, their communities and sometimes the entire world.

One of the most inspiring orations ever given in American history was Dr. Martin Luther King's famous speech, "I've Been to the Mountaintop," delivered in the middle of the Memphis Sanitation Workers Strike at Mason Temple in Memphis, Tennessee, on April 3, 1968, the day before his assassination. He said,

> Well, I don't know what will happen now. We've got some difficult days ahead. But it doesn't matter with me now. Because I've been to the mountaintop. And I don't mind. Like anybody, I would like to live a long life. Longevity has its place. But I'm not concerned about that now. I just want to do God's will.[1]

Dr. King had a clear focus for his life—to fulfill God's will. Attention to the concept of fulfilling the will of God seems to fluctuate from decade to decade. When I was in college in the 1970s, it was an important concept for young Christians. Henrietta Mears led an incredible Christian education renaissance in California during the 1930s, 1940s and 1950s. In her "Ten Commandments as a Sunday School Teacher," the fifth commandment was: "I will seek to help each one discover the will of God, because the Master can use every talent."[2] Unfortunately, there has been little conversation in the American church about "the will of God" during the past two decades. I believe it is a core biblical concept that Christian leaders need to elevate to the center of their thinking.

C. S. Lewis cuts through the clutter regarding the will of God when he quotes the English author Joseph Addison in chapter 10 of Lewis's book *A Preface to Paradise Lost*:

> The great moral which reigns in Milton is the most universal and the most useful that can be imagined—that obedience to the will of God makes people happy, and disobedience makes them miserable.[3]

Most Christian leaders, by nature, focus on fulfilling God's will for their own life but spend little time helping the people they lead to discover and fulfill God's will for their lives. A leader, by definition, is people-focused—without people, you lead no one. When you understand leadership as helping others fulfill God's will for their lives, the conversation changes. The question becomes, "How can I help you fulfill God's purpose for your life?" Once the spotlight is off of you and focused on others, your leadership possibilities and potential will explode! You will experience a river of fresh water flowing through you to others.

Christian leaders help others accomplish God's will by calling them to follow Jesus in all aspects of their lives. Slowly read and meditate on these verses that focus on the biblical call to fulfill God's will:

♦ "Your kingdom come, your will be done, on earth as it is in heaven" (Mt 6:10).

♦ "Then I said, 'Behold, I have come to do your will, O God, as it is written of me in the scroll of the book'" (Heb 10:7 ESV, referring to Jesus).

♦ "Going a little farther, [Jesus] fell with his face to the ground and prayed, 'My Father, if it is possible, may this cup be taken from me. Yet not as I will, but as you will'" (Mt 26:39).

♦ "Therefore do not be foolish, but understand what the Lord's will is" (Eph 5:17).

♦ "As servants of Christ, doing the will of God from the heart, rendering service with a good will as to the Lord" (Eph 6:6-7 ESV).

♦ "We have not stopped praying for you. We continually ask God to fill you with the knowledge of his will through all the wisdom and understanding that the Spirit gives" (Col 1:9).

♦ "Then you will be able to test and approve what God's will is—his good, pleasing and perfect will" (Rom 12:2).

♦ "The world and its desires pass away, but whoever does the will of God lives forever" (1 Jn 2:17).

Since a good and effective leader helps others to fulfill God's will for their lives, it follows that *every Christian is a leader in someone else's life*. For example, I want to help my wife, Shelly, fulfill God's will for her life while she also acts as a leader in my life, helping me fulfill God's will. Together, Shelly and I are leaders to our four children, earnestly desiring to help each child hear God's special call so that, in their own unique ways, they can fulfill his will. Now that all our children are adults, I hope that each of them will be a leader to Shelly and myself, continuing to help us hear God's call.

Here is a sequence of four questions every Christian leader should ask:

♦ What is God's calling and will for me right now? How am I to live this out? How does the Holy Spirit want to help me grow as a leader?

♦ What is God's calling and will for the church or organization I am a part of? How will the leaders and members of this organization discover this?

♦ How can I as a leader help everyone in our church or organization to understand their calling in life and how they can serve God?

♦ How does a clear understanding of God's will determine the ways in which we will minister to our community and world?

A second misunderstanding is that Christian leadership emanates from either force of personality or positional power. Is this how Jesus understood leadership? Consider these verses:

Jesus called them together and said, "You know that the rulers of the Gentiles lord it over them, and their high officials exercise authority over them. Not so with you. Instead, whoever wants to become great among you must be your servant, and whoever wants to be first must be your slave—just as the Son of Man did not come to be served, but to serve, and to give his life as a ransom for many." (Mt 20:25-28)

Jesus was very clear that his followers should not adopt the leadership methods of the Romans. Roman leaders relied on two sources for leadership power: position and force of personality. Their title or rank conferred on them power, and the force of their personality magnified that power. Jesus instructed his followers to carefully observe the Roman leaders and then choose to lead in a different manner.

This then is the second principle of Christian leadership for a follower of Jesus:

The biblical way of leadership development is to allow the foundations of your life—your character, gifts, passions, personality and habits—to grow strong. Then you can lead from the depths of how God has created, gifted and formed you. The presence and authority of a Christian leader is derived from strength in spirituality, chemistry, strategy and leadership wisdom.

One of the primary themes in J. R. R. Tolkien's *The Lord of the Rings* is the lure of power and its ability to corrupt and destroy leaders who seek to possess that power. Writer Tim Chester comments:

> At the heart of the story is the ring and it is the ring of power. *The Lord of the Rings* is a story about power. And it is a story about the corrupting nature of power. The ring symbolizes power. And the ring corrupts those who come into contact with it. It deceives and it ensnares. Above all, humanity—"the race of men" as the book keeps calling them—cannot be trusted with power.[4]

Abraham Lincoln cautioned, "Nearly all men can stand adversity, but if you want to test a man's character, give him power." Often Christian leaders subconsciously believe that they should use the force of their own personality to lead. They believe that something within their personality, intelligence or charisma is so influential and important that this gives them the right and calling to lead.

Other Christian leaders feel entitled to lead through the position they have attained in an organization. Their title and role is the defining aspect of their leadership identity, rather than their calling and gifting by God. As John Maxwell said, "A great leader's courage to fulfill his vision comes from passion, not position."[5] Neither of these two ways of acquiring leadership is healthy.

Listen to these words of the apostle Paul regarding Jesus-style leadership:

> In your relationships with one another, have the same mindset as Christ Jesus: Who, being in very nature God, did not consider equality with God something to be used to his own advantage; rather, he made himself nothing by taking the very nature of a servant, being made in human likeness. (Phil 2:5-7)

We have been chosen, called and gifted by God for a life of service, and we are commanded to minister in the Spirit, not in the flesh. Jesus calls us to a new way of leading. Godly Christian leaders are formed through God's deepening and purifying work. They are shaped by God, who forms within them qualities of godliness, wisdom, knowledge, humility, strength, confidence, power and love, through the action of the Holy Spirit. True leadership is based on your identity in Christ, God's specific calling and purpose for your life and the expectation of the empowerment of God, working through the Holy Spirit. Christian leaders can then minister with presence and authority in Holy Spirit confidence.

TWO PRECONDITIONS FOR CHRISTIAN LEADERSHIP

In addition to the two principles described above, there are also two preconditions that qualify a leader who wishes to lead as Jesus led.

The first precondition for fruitful leadership is self-awareness.

Most people believe that self-awareness is about their own evaluation of themselves. It is not! Self-awareness is revealed in your ability to "stand apart" from yourself and receive feedback on how *others* experience you. Unfortunately, if the truth be told, most of us are rather delusional about who we really are. We view ourselves from an "insider" perspective and cannot achieve an objective mindset. In most cases, those around you can give you much more accurate feedback about who you really are.

Without self-awareness, Christian leaders can become toxic, controlling and destructive. Have you ever met a Christian leader like that? Many Christian leaders create protective environments that allow them to hide from the truth of how people experience them. In contrast, seekers of truth learn to view themselves as others perceive them. Increased self-awareness is an important step in allowing God to transform you and your way of leading.

The second precondition for fruitful leadership is teachability. If you want to know if a person is teachable, just listen to whether or not he or she asks good questions.

Teachability will increase your capacity to understand yourself, others and the world around you. Teachability is best revealed in your ability to ask incisive questions of others, including questions about yourself, and allow the answers to shape your self-perception, thinking and behavior.

Teachability is the willingness to change based on other peoples' valid input and the convicting work of the Holy Spirit. The simplest way to grow in teachability is to ask wise leaders probing questions about what they have learned as a leader and what advice they might have for your growth. Teachability requires the willingness to be vulnerable; you will hear things about yourself that you will not want to hear, but that is the price required for growth in leadership. Teachability is one of the most powerful tools God uses to form Christian leaders.

In Numbers 12:3, Moses is identified as "a very humble man, more humble than anyone else on the face of the earth." An example of his humility and teachability was when he asked his father-in-law, Jethro, to teach him how to better lead his people. Have you ever asked your mother-in-law or father-in-law for leadership advice? What an amazing level of teachability!

How can you identify teachable people? It is simple. Teachable people love asking questions, especially questions that invite honest observations about themselves and the reality of their situation. Author Max DePree wrote, "The first responsibility of a leader is to define reality."[6] The best practice for Christian leaders to follow in order to understand their reality is to ask questions. What percentage of Christian leaders are good at asking questions—10 percent? Maybe 20 percent?

Have you ever noticed that Jesus was one of the best question-askers ever? Did you know that Jesus asked 140 questions in the Gospels? Here is Jesus' most famous two-pronged question:

Jesus and his disciples went on to the villages around Caesarea Philippi. On the way he asked them, "Who do people say I am?" They replied, "Some say John the Baptist; others say Elijah; and still others, one of the prophets." "But what about you?" he asked. "Who do you say I am?" Peter answered, "You are the Messiah." (Mk 8:27-29)

"Who do people say I am?" What a great first question! What an open-ended conversation starter! The question created an exceptional way to engage his followers regarding how the crowd experienced him.

The first question then set up the second question to the disciples: "But what about you? Who do you say I am?" The disciples were not allowed to just talk about what others thought about Jesus. Instead, he used the second question to focus in on the real issue for all people in all times: "Who do you think I am?" To his disciples he said, "Don't answer for anyone else. Tell me who *you* think I am."

Your goal as a Christian leader is to help other people fulfill God's will for their lives. Rather than achieving this through your own power and position, it is accomplished through drawing on your gifts, personality, passions, habits and character, aided by the work of the Holy Spirit. God's ability to change and transform you into a better leader increases exponentially when you are aware of how other people experience you. Self-awareness increases by being teachable, and teachability is developed through asking incisive questions. You will never be an outstanding Christian leader without understanding these two preconditions.

The rest of this book is dedicated to providing you with the understanding, models and tools you will need to grow stronger as a Christian leader. I hope you find it an energizing and challenging adventure!

MISSION ASSIGNMENT—LEADING AS JESUS LED

1. "Leadership is helping other people fulfill God's will for their lives." Is this a helpful definition? How would following this definition change you as a Christian leader?

2. "The biblical way of leadership development is to allow the foundations of your life—your character, gifts, passions, personality and habits—to grow strong." How important is character in your life? What habits do you have that help you live a life of integrity?

3. What specific habits do you have that ensure you receive regular feedback about how others experience you? This is a rather dangerous activity!

4. "Teachable people love asking questions, especially questions that invite honest observations about themselves and the reality of their situation." On a scale of 1 to 10, how good are you at asking incisive questions? What keeps you from doing this? How can you improve?

4

Your Gifts, Passions
and Personality

A winner is someone who recognizes his God-given talents,
works his tail off to develop them into skills, and uses
these skills to accomplish his goals.

Larry Bird

Shortly after my fiftieth birthday I felt a desire to buy a different kind of car. For most of my adult life, I drove rather conventional vehicles, but this time I wanted something different. I wanted to buy a convertible, and I knew exactly which one I wanted. Thirty years earlier, I had spent each summer of college as a door-to-door book salesman. It was difficult, emotionally taxing work, but if you could survive it was financially rewarding. We were required to work a minimum of seventy-five hours a week, excluding Sunday. The check I received at the end of my third summer was large enough that I could buy a brand new car. My friend Jim Johnson and I went to the local Audi dealer, whose new model, the Audi Fox, had just received three "Car of the Year" awards. My heart was set on buying one.

We drove to the dealership and entered the showroom dressed in jeans and jean jackets, with long hair and sideburns. For fifteen minutes we saw the sales force on the other side of the room, but not one would venture over to talk to us. They assumed we were penniless hippies. We finally left and went next door to the Toyota dealership, where the sales staff greeted us warmly. Within an hour I had purchased a brand new, shiny, 1974 Toyota Celica. As it turned out, the Audi Fox was one of the most mechanically deficient cars ever built. In contrast, my Celica ran perfectly for 150,000 miles until I sold it—quite a feat in those days. Most important, it was the car I drove when I picked up the young lady who would be the love of my life, my wife, Shelly.

I always thought that Toyota's 1993 to 1999 Celica model was one of the best-looking small convertibles ever. I decided that buying one after my fiftieth birthday would fuel our romance as we could blissfully cruised together around Lake Minnetonka during the twenty-seven warm days of the Minnesota summer. I scoured the want ads and found a 1997 for sale ten miles west of our house. Without mentioning a word to my wife, my youngest daughter and I drove out to see it. It was black and in perfect condition—I could hear it calling out my name. I made an instant decision to buy it, and the next day, Kate and I drove my "new" car home, top down, popping the clutch, accelerating through each corner, fresh air blowing through our hair. We finally cornered into our driveway to the surprise of Shelly.

If you love driving a car like I do, this simple analogy may help you visualize the relationship of the three qualities that determine the unique way you minister for Christ—your *gifts*, your *passions* and your *personality*. Your gifts are the vehicle that you drive; your passions are the gas in the vehicle's tank; and your personality determines how you drive. The more clarity you have about your gifts, passions and personality, the more fulfilled and fruitful you will be as you lead as God has formed you.

Just as I wanted to buy a car that fit my passions and personality, God uses your gifts, passions and personality to give focus, power and dimension to your leadership.

UNDERSTANDING YOUR INDIVIDUAL STRENGTHS

As I have led thousands of pastors and lay people through the Leadership Stool model, I have discovered that virtually every person is able to identify his or her strongest leg. For many, it is a revelation; it gives words and a voice to something they perhaps subconsciously knew but could not articulate. It is such a joy to watch their eyes light up and hear them exclaim, "Yes, God has gifted me in spirituality (or chemistry or strategy)." Most Christians do not live with a clear understanding of how they are gifted, nor of how they should serve God. My heart leaps when I hear a Christian say, "Now I know how God can use me!"

Gifts. God has given every Christian a special gift with which to serve him, either spirituality, chemistry or strategy. This is the vehicle you drive. For most, instinct, ability and probably passion come naturally in that leg. God has already given people many of the skills needed to use their strongest leg, and it will produce most of their ministry fruit. We experience joy, fulfill God's will and produce fruit when we use this gift. We feel fulfilled serving in this area. Use of our strongest leg will cause us to feel the pleasure of God and experience thankfulness toward the giver of all good gifts.

Do you realize how critical this is—how important it is for all Christians to know how God has wired them, and how their gifts, passions and personality can produce fruitfulness and fulfillment?

God created each person with gifts to be used for his glory and the good of the world. It is important that each Christian identify and use his or her gifts, because this is one of the means by which God redeems and restores his creation. Often, however, Christians deny their gifts, ignore them, diminish them or misuse them. Have you ever done this?

In 1 Peter 4:10, Peter encourages Christians to use the gifts God has given them: "Each of you should use whatever gift you have received to serve others, as faithful stewards of God's grace in its various forms."

Your gifts are from God, and identifying them is the first step in understanding how to be fruitful in ministry and leadership. God also gave you passions and a personality, which differ in nature from gifts. They are not given in full bloom but unfold over time. Passions and personality are given by God but also shaped by your family of origin and your personal experiences.

Passions. Passion is the gas in your tank. Passions are what excite you, what move you; passions are the well of your physical, emotional and spiritual energy. Good leaders are moved with passion about what they believe and what they want to see happen in the world. Passions can grow over time, yet many of your passions were apparent when you were still a child or adolescent.

Personality. Personality is how you drive the car. It is made up of the characteristic patterns of thoughts, feelings and behaviors that make you unique. Personalities differ greatly between individuals and strongly affect how you lead and serve.

I have discovered that each of the six leadership styles that I'll discuss in section three is populated by people with similar gifts, passions and personalities. They are created by God to lead similarly to other leaders with the same leadership style.

In summary, your leadership ability will grow as you understand, strengthen and use your gifts; allow more and more of the God-given part of your personality and passions to emerge; let God set you free from the parts of your personality and passions that are self-centered and destructive; and develop personal habits that strengthen and reinforce spirituality, chemistry, strategy and leadership wisdom.

Section 3 will help you identify which of the six Christian leadership styles God has given you. You will discover there that your gifts, passions and personality work together in harmony to produce the type of leader that you are.

MISSION ASSIGNMENT—HABITS AND TIME INVESTMENT

As well as understanding your gifts, passions and personality, it is vitally important that Christian leaders develop personal habits that strengthen and reinforce the development of spirituality, chemistry, strategy and leadership wisdom. The simplest way to understand the true measure of your habits is to determine the amount of time that you spend performing each activity daily—and whether that time investment reflects your true priorities.

Intentions become reality through habits. A daily regimen of good leadership habits, like exercise, will produce health, balance, integrity and wholeness. Typically leaders spend most of their ministry time using their strongest leg, less time using their intermediate leg and little time using their weakest leg. Imagine what changes would occur if you developed a more balanced use of each leg. Doing this would quickly improve your leadership.

For most people, good habits require accountability. If left to ourselves, we tend to spend most of our time on what we enjoy and what comes easiest, and little time on what we don't like. We seldom take into account the importance of each activity when we determine the amount of time we spend on any given task—even though we may recognize that our lax habits are diminishing our fruitfulness for Christ. Strong leaders develop habits that reflect their true priorities. If you want to become a better leader, you will need to be vigilant in monitoring your habits and let your time investment match your priorities. A quote often attributed to Abraham Lincoln (probably erroneously) refers to preparation and habits: "Give me six hours to chop down a tree and I will spend the first four sharpening the axe."

In summary, focus on your call from God, which can be discerned through listening to God's voice, is accompanied by the confirmation of the body of Christ, and will be in alignment with your natural and spiritual gifts. Your call is expressed and magnified by your passions and personality, which become part of your life and schedule through your habits of work, connection, learning and character. And all of this is proven through fruit, which can be defined as human activity touched by the Spirit of God. Make sure you pray for, watch for and then count the fruit!

1. What are the personal and professional habits that you need to change so that they more truly reflect your priorities in life?

2. Who is the trusted colleague, mentor or friend that you could establish an accountability relationship with regarding your habits and time investment?

SECTION ONE ONLINE ACTIVITY: *IMPROVING TEAM DYNAMICS*

The leaders who work most effectively, it seems to me, never say "I."
And that's not because they have trained themselves not to say "I."
They don't think "I." They think "we"; they think "team." They
understand their job to be to make the team function. They accept
responsibility and don't sidestep it, but "we" gets the credit.

PETER F. DRUCKER,
MANAGING THE NON-PROFIT ORGANIZATION

While the Leadership Stool model will help you grow stronger as a leader, it is equally valuable because of how it will help you build strong teams in your church or organization. It will improve their connections with one another, strengthen their appreciation for one another's gifts, and help the team develop more unity and productivity.

I was invited to meet with the pastoral staff of a prominent megachurch in Southern California. There were fifteen pastors present as I explained the three legs of Christian leadership. Then they each identified which leg was their strongest. Eight were strongest in chemistry, seven in strategy and zero in spirituality. With a surprised look on my face, I asked them whether they noticed anything wrong with their staff profile. Nope. Not one found it unusual that there was not one leader on their team who was strongest in spirituality. I looked at them with amazement, knowing that they were missing one-third of a complete profile. Each staff person was very gifted, but together they were not a balanced team.

Another team, the board of a Christian organization, took the online team profile. Out of the twelve members, nine were strongest in spirituality, two in chemistry and one in strategy. The organization's leader immediately knew what to do—begin a process to make sure the newly elected board members helped balance the team. His motivation to change came from realizing that their profile immediately explained the deficiencies in the organization—the board excelled at loving Jesus, but they did not get as much accomplished in the physical world of ministry transformation.

Greg was one of the first leaders to have his leadership team take the online team inventory. He scheduled an overnight weekend retreat, inviting both the leadership team and their spouses, to process what this leadership model meant for how the team ministered, as well as its significance for their marriages. Here were my four follow-up questions for Greg after the retreat and his responses:

Q: What did the retreat do for you as the pastor?

A: It was a wonderful tool to help more people move toward the center of our team, both those who have been there for a while and those who are new.

Q: What did it do for your lay leaders?

A: It validated their sense of importance; it reinforced the impact they have made to our church; it helped them better understand leadership; and it authenticated their contribution to the leadership of our team.

Q: What did it do for their marriages?

A: By having spouses there, it became an opportunity to give back to our leaders and provide a blessing to their marriage. It helped them know each other better. We saw a healthy wholeness in our couples. The spouses were very engaged in the discussion. They helped take us further in conversation, and it became a better dialogue.

Q: What did it do for the team dynamics?

A: This tool is different from any other personality test I have taken. It is the spirituality component that is so different. It helps me as a pastor lead from that place. In many church leadership structures, spirituality is a given and is often relegated to the sidelines. The outsiders and unbelievers that end up coming to our church don't actually think that churches are spiritual enough. The leadership model validated our church's existence. Prayer and fasting are very normal activities in our church. This tool can be very helpful for younger churches like ours, especially those that came out of a context where deep spirituality was lacking.

Not only will this exercise help the team see and value the diverse gifts of one another, but also additional online resources can provide each leader with a plan to become a wiser, stronger and better leader (see "Section Two Online Activity").

Sign up for the Leadership Team Inventory and have each member of your staff, board or committee take the online "Team Profile Tool" two to three weeks before your meeting or retreat. Each person will receive his or her own report instantly, and the leader will receive a four-page team report. This report is written as a discovery tool to help your team walk through the strengths of each person on the team and what it means for that team to appreciate and best use the gifts of everyone. There is a workbook available at the Six Style store to use while facilitating the group discovery process.

Please go to sixstyles.org/teamprofiles.php for more information and to register for your team profile. There is a nominal charge for the team profile.

LEADERSHIP
STRENGTH

Section Two provides a detailed explanation of each of the three legs and the seat of this leadership model. It identifies love as the foundation for God's transformation of your leadership. Spirituality, chemistry, strategy and leadership wisdom are unpacked through examining the message and mission of Jesus. This section will give you a practical and biblical understanding of the core foundations of Christian leadership.

5

Love Changes Everything

The greatest disease in the West today is not TB or leprosy; it is being unwanted, unloved, and uncared for. We can cure physical diseases with medicine, but the only cure for loneliness, despair, and hopelessness is love. . . . The poverty in the West is a different kind of poverty—it is not only a poverty of loneliness but also of spirituality. There's a hunger for love, as there is a hunger for God.

Mother Teresa

At first glance, a person might think that the first step to becoming stronger in spirituality would be exerting more effort in becoming more spiritual. In the same way, increased strength in chemistry would require exerting more effort in human relationships. And to get stronger in strategy, the first step would be to exert more effort on better planning and organization. The problem with that type of thinking is that it views these leadership qualities as commodities. "If only I can acquire more of that commodity, I will become a better leader."

In life, we often find that we receive what we need not by focusing on the need itself but by seeking an underlying quality that is much more important. Jesus was very specific about this:

> Therefore I tell you, do not worry about your life, what you will eat or drink; or about your body, what you will wear. Is not life more than food, and the body more than clothes? . . . So do not

worry, saying, "What shall we eat?" or "What shall we drink?"
or "What shall we wear?" For the pagans run after all these
things, and your heavenly Father knows that you need them. But
seek first his kingdom and his righteousness, and all these things
will be given to you as well. (Mt 6:25, 31-33)

This is definitely the case with spirituality, chemistry and strategy. To
understand the critical elements underlying each, we need to remember
what these three terms truly mean. *Spirituality* encompasses all that it
means to love God; *chemistry* encompasses all that it means to love
people; *strategy* encompasses all that it means to love the mission of God
in the world. The key focus and answer to growth in these three critical
arenas is the word *love*. Love is what produces a life that is other-focused
rather than self-centered. Growth in spirituality, chemistry and strategy
should occur by God's love transforming you from the inside out.

THE THREE LEGS OF LEADERSHIP

A simple way to understand spirituality, chemistry and strategy is to
compare the three words in each row of table 5.1 that describe spirituality, chemistry and strategy.

Table 5.1. The Three Legs of Leadership

Spirituality	Chemistry	Strategy
Loving God	Loving people	Loving the world
Great Commandment A	Great Commandment B	Great Commission
Receiving the vision	Rallying around the vision	Implementing the vision
Praying together	Playing together	Planning together
Spirit	Heart	Mind
Higher up	Deeper in	Further out
Eyes of faith	Hearts of love	Hands to work
Spiritual intelligence	Emotional intelligence	Strategic intelligence
Power	Unity	Alignment
Surrender	Gather	Advance
Sanctuary	Fellowship hall	Board room

Past orientation	Present orientation	Future orientation
Pulpit	Coffee cup	Whiteboard
Beauty	Goodness	Truth
Christ	Community	Cause

*Special thanks to John Wenrich for creating this table.

This chapter will help you focus on love by reflecting on three principles, each followed by a short commentary, an illustrative Scripture and a prayer.

SPIRITUALITY

Principle

If spirituality is your weakest leg, you won't become more spiritual by exerting human effort to increase your spirituality. Instead, you become more spiritual by cultivating habits that allow you to more fully experience God's love for you, and then letting that love focus, deepen and strengthen your spirituality.

Commentary

A person becomes strong in spirituality by loving God. The source and wellspring of loving God is the experience of receiving love from God. Because everyone experiences guilt, shame, trials and sometimes neglect in life, many Christians never truly comprehend or experience the lavish love of God. They have trouble believing that the God of the universe loves them with an extravagant love.

Scripture

I pray that out of his glorious riches he may strengthen you with power through his Spirit in your inner being, so that Christ may dwell in your hearts through faith. And I pray that you, being rooted and established in love, may have power, together with all the Lord's holy people, to grasp how wide and long and high and deep is the love of Christ, and to know this love that surpasses knowledge—that you may be filled to the measure of all the fullness of God. (Eph 3:16-19)

Prayer

O the deep, deep love of Jesus, vast, unmeasured, boundless, free!
Rolling as a mighty ocean in its fullness over me!
Underneath me, all around me, is the current of thy love—
leading onward, leading homeward to thy glorious rest above!
(Samuel Trevor Francis, "O the Deep, Deep Love of Jesus")

CHEMISTRY

Principle

If chemistry is your weakest leg, you won't become stronger in chemistry by exerting human effort to increase it. Instead, as you cultivate habits that enable you to experience God's love for people in a more profound way, your chemistry will grow stronger.

Commentary

We grow in love for others by understanding the implications of the gospel in a deeper way, and its message of love, mercy, compassion and grace. You do this by imbibing the words of Jesus, Paul and other biblical authors that encourage the demonstration of the fruits of the Spirit.

Scripture

You, my brothers and sisters, were called to be free. But do not use your freedom to indulge the flesh; rather, serve one another humbly in love. For the entire law is fulfilled in keeping this one command: "Love your neighbor as yourself." . . . The fruit of the Spirit is love, joy, peace, forbearance, kindness, goodness, faithfulness, gentleness and self-control. Against such things there is no law. (Gal 5:13-14, 22-23)

Prayer

Thank you, Lord, for the gift of your Spirit. As I walk in love and in the Holy Spirit, allow the fruits of the Spirit to be revealed in my life as something inviting and delectable.

STRATEGY

Principle
If strategy is your weakest leg, you won't become stronger in it by exerting human effort to become more strategic. Instead, you will become stronger in strategy as you let God's love for the world focus, deepen and strengthen your strategy.

Commentary
Our love for the world grows when we understand in a deeper way how the compassionate, inviting and limitless love of God drives his mission in our world, and how the apostles and subsequent Christian leaders let love motivate them as they prayed over, planned, organized and implemented that mission.

Scripture
But you will receive power when the Holy Spirit comes on you; and you will be my witnesses in Jerusalem, and in all Judea and Samaria, and to the ends of the earth. (Acts 1:8)

Now get up and stand on your feet. I have appeared to you to appoint you as a servant and as a witness of what you have seen and will see of me. I will rescue you from your own people and from the Gentiles. I am sending you to them to open their eyes and turn them from darkness to light, and from the power of Satan to God, so that they may receive forgiveness of sins and a place among those who are sanctified by faith in me. (Acts 26:16-18)

Prayer
God, we follow in the footsteps of those who through faith conquered kingdoms, administered justice and gained what was promised. Give us love, vision, faith and courage as we tell and act out the mission and message of Jesus in our world.

One of the most moving stories of how love changes everything is the relationship between secular journalist Malcolm Muggeridge and Mother Teresa. She was instrumental in Muggeridge's coming to faith.

While watching her receding into the distance aboard a train at a Calcutta station, Muggeridge wrote, "When the train began to move and I walked away, I felt as though I were leaving behind me all the beauty and all the joy of the universe. Something of God's universal love has rubbed off on Mother Teresa, giving her homely features a notable luminosity; a shining quality."[1]

MISSION ASSIGNMENT—STRENGTHENING YOUR TWELVE CORE FOUNDATIONS

I've noticed at my fitness center that there is an increased emphasis on strengthening core muscles. Core exercises train the muscles in four areas: your lower back, hips, pelvis and abdomen, so that they can work together in harmony. Strong core muscles create a powerful foundation at the center of your body that increases back strength, improves performance and leads to better balance and stability on both the playing field and in daily activities.

For a Christian leader, there are also "core muscles" (referred to here as *core foundations*) for each of the four leadership areas: spirituality, chemistry, strategy and leadership wisdom. The next four chapters will help you learn how to strengthen yourself in each of these core foundations.

1. What do you think might be three core foundations (for example, prayer) that would strengthen your spirituality?

2. What do you think might be three core foundations that would strengthen your chemistry?

3. What do you think might be three core foundations that would strengthen your strategy?

4. What do you think might be three core foundations that would strengthen your leadership wisdom?

6

Love God

Strengthening Your Spirituality

God made us: invented us as a man invents an engine. A car is made to run on petrol, and it would not run properly on anything else. Now God designed the human machine to run on Himself. He Himself is the fuel our spirits were designed to burn, or the food our spirits were designed to feed on. There is no other.

C. S. Lewis

SPIRITUALITY FOCUSES ON LOVING GOD WITH ALL YOUR HEART.

♦ The core emphasis of spirituality is summed up in the verse, "Love the Lord your God with all your heart and with all your soul and with all your mind and with all your strength" (Mk 12:30).

♦ Spirituality is demonstrated to us in the relationship Jesus had with his Father.

♦ People grow in spirituality as they receive God's love for themselves, love him in return and become all they are created to be in Christ.

Prayer

Lord, create in me a heart to love you. Burn out of my soul everything that causes me to place myself above you or separates me from you. Fill my heart with love for you and with joy and passion for the deep things of God.

Leaders who are strong in spirituality have an inborn instinct to love God. They are committed to deep spiritual transformation that produces the life-changing work of God in themselves. Leaders who are strongest in spirituality focus first on their relationship with God. Their ministry flows out of this vital, life-giving friendship. God uses them to create a spiritual atmosphere in their relationships and their church or organization. They are designed by God to communicate the importance of living in the realm of the Spirit. Those who are strong in spirituality want others to grow deeper in relationship with God and be formed by his Spirit. Their passion is that the Spirit of God and the story of Jesus transform people from broken, alienated humans into daughters and sons of God. They focus on the "what and why"—what God did for us, and why God did it. They hope to connect everyone with the God who created a beautiful and wondrous world, filled with love and peace, who longs to redeem and restore them, and all creation, from the destructive power of sin and evil.

People strongest in spirituality hope to communicate what God has done for us in Christ. They emphasize a life founded in the Scriptures, which provides a roadmap to guide us in our journey with God. They also emphasize that our growth in Christ is both an individual and a communal activity.

Spirituality people experience joy and fruitfulness when they do the following:

◆ teach children and adults the Bible

◆ encourage individual and corporate prayer

◆ practice healing prayer

◆ follow and teach the spiritual disciplines

◆ lead spiritual retreats

◆ mentor and disciple teens and adults one on one

◆ encourage confession and repentance

◆ pray for and seek the presence and filling of the Holy Spirit

- encourage spiritual honesty
- provide spiritual direction
- model saturation in the Scriptures
- promote a robust walk with God
- live with genuine humility
- foster peace

THE THREE CORE FOUNDATIONS OF SPIRITUALITY

The leg of spirituality has three core foundations. In order to grow deeper in spirituality, it is necessary to invest a significant amount of time and energy strengthening each core foundation.

Saturation in Scripture. The first core foundation is saturation in Scripture. The early Christians in Berea demonstrated this immersion in God's Word in Acts 17:11: "Now the Berean Jews were of more noble character than those in Thessalonica, for they received the message with great eagerness and examined the Scriptures every day to see if what Paul said was true." A person builds this foundation by passionately pursuing truth and wisdom from the Scriptures. According to Biblica (formerly the International Bible Society), there is currently a precipitous downward trend in Bible reading. Their research shows that every year in America, one quarter of a million people give up reading the Bible. Individuals who are 18 to 29 years old read the Bible less often and with less interest than older generations. Nine out of ten people say that the one thing they most need out of their church is help studying the Bible in depth, yet 80 percent are not getting it from their church.[1] To grow in spirituality we need to continually saturate our hearts and minds in the words of Scripture.

While the trends are discouraging, the resources available for scriptural saturation today are amazing. YouVersion, the most popular Bible app in the world, has had over 100 million people download this online Bible to their smart device. At present, they have 719 translations of the Bible available, representing 419 languages! You can read or listen to the Bible in any place, at any time, in any way you wish. There are also other outstanding Bible resources available, both in print and online.

In John 6:68-69, Peter told Jesus, "Lord, to whom shall we go? You have the words of eternal life. We have come to believe and to know that you are the Holy One of God." The foundation of spirituality is built on knowing the words of eternal life, which come from living a life immersed in the Word of God.

I have noticed that Christian leaders who live a life saturated in Scripture incorporate many of the following five habits into their daily practices. The first habit is living a life of biblical insight and passion. The Bible was not meant for rote reading and learning. Instead, it is God's living Word to us and should inspire, convict and challenge us, giving us a growing passion for God. In the book *Shaped by the Word*, M. Robert Mulholland describes how we are meant to read the Bible in a way that will transform us:

> It is to allow the text to master you. In reading the Bible, this means we come to the text with an openness to hear, to receive, to respond, to be a servant of the Word, rather than a master of the text. Such openness requires an abandonment of the false self and its habitual temptation to control the text for its own purposes. . . . You seek to allow the text to become that intrusion of the Word of God into your life, to address you, to encounter you at deeper levels of your being.[2]

The second habit is reading or listening to the Bible systematically. Online audio Bibles can be so helpful for accomplishing this. When you take a walk, go for a bike ride (only one ear bud, please!) or sit alone in your office, you are in a perfect setting to listen to the Bible. Third, for Scripture to create genuine life transformation, it is necessary to go deeper in your study of the Bible. I use an iPhone app called "SpeakIt," which reads aloud any online document. This lets me listen aloud to the many thoughtful biblical articles found on the Internet. The fourth habit is consistent theological reading and reflection. I try to focus on going deeper with wise and learned authors who have been formative in my life, such as C. S. Lewis, N. T. Wright and Dorothy Sayers. The fifth habit is listening to God's voice through the Scriptures. Reading, studying and reflecting is not enough; prayerfully asking God to speak to you through the Bible will let God transform your life through the Holy Spirit. Christians have always been people of the book, reveling in the story, the wonder and the glory of God, as revealed to us on the pages of Scripture.

Spiritual disciplines. The second core foundation is spiritual disciplines. These habits reflect a consistent, vital walk with Jesus, marked by the disciplines of prayer, devotional reading, worship, fasting, obedience, service and spiritual retreats.

Scripture presents Jesus as our model here, one who understood the need to spend time in the presence of his Father. These seven spiritual disciplines help strengthen our relationship with God and cause us to grow deeper in intimacy with him. All require a quiet slowing down of the pace of life and a recognition that they are called disciplines because they allow God to lovingly train, correct, mold and perfect us.

Sensitivity to the Holy Spirit. The third core foundation is sensitivity to the Holy Spirit. In order for a Christian leader to be sensitive to the Spirit, he or she needs to walk humbly with God, listen and respond to his voice and be filled daily with the Holy Spirit. Sensitivity to the Holy Spirit helps us keep our ear tuned to his whispers, nudges, convictions, promptings and directions.

It is helpful to remember three D-words when asking the Holy Spirit to fill our lives with wisdom. The first word is *discernment.* The Holy Spirit can give us unique understanding in each situation that we deal with, so that we can perceive God's life-giving way. As Ruth Haley Barton describes it, "Discernment is first of all a habit, a way of seeing that eventually permeates our whole life. It is the journey from spiritual blindness (not seeing God anywhere or seeing him only where we expect to see him) to spiritual sight (finding God everywhere, especially where we least expect it)."[3]

The second is *deliverance.* This is what we need when we face the battles within and without, which most of us experience daily. The Holy Spirit can help us overcome temptation by showing us a way of escape that allows us to follow Jesus instead.

The third is *direction*. The Holy Spirit will lead and guide us in the specific way we should go. All ministry that lasts has to be done in the power and direction of the Holy Spirit, because only the Spirit can produce lasting fruit.

THE SPIRITUALITY EXAMEN

An examen is a spiritual discipline that asks a series of probing questions in the presence of God, with the reader seeking to be as direct, honest and transparent as possible before him. Spend some time slowly reading through this spirituality examen and answer the questions placed before you.

Today, I commit myself to loving God with all my heart by growing in the three core foundations of spirituality.

Opening prayer. Lord, create in me a heart to love you. Burn out of my soul everything that keeps me from you and keeps me placing myself above you. Fill me with love in my heart toward you, so that I may be filled with joy and passion for the deep things of God.

Am I living a life saturated in Scripture?

◆ Am I living a life filled with biblical insight and passion?

◆ Am I reading and listening to the Bible systematically?

◆ Am I daily studying the Scriptures?

◆ Am I reading and reflecting on substantive theological works?

◆ Am I listening to God's voice through the Scriptures?

Am I living a life marked by devotional practices and spiritual disciplines?

◆ Am I nurturing a consistent, vital walk with Jesus?

◆ Do I practice disciplines of

   • prayer?

   • devotional reading?

   • worship?

- fasting?
- service?
- obedience?
- spiritual retreats?

Am I living a life marked by sensitivity to the Holy Spirit?

♦ Do I view myself more highly than I should, or do I walk humbly with God?

♦ Am I living a life filled with humility and attention to the voice of the Spirit?

♦ Do I listen and respond to the voice and leading of the Holy Spirit?

♦ Am I seeking daily to be filled and directed by the Spirit?

Concluding prayer. Thank you, O God. Fill me with a thirst for your Scriptures. Fill me with the desire to commune with you by dwelling in your presence. And help me to depend on the direction and voice of the Holy Spirit. Amen.

MISSION ASSIGNMENT—THE THREE FOUNDATIONS OF SPIRITUALITY

Rate yourself in the three core foundations of spirituality, giving a 1 to the foundation you consider your strongest, a 2 to the intermediate foundation and a 3 to the weakest foundation. Then write down the name of a Christian leader you personally know who has been a role model for you of strength in each foundation.

Table 6.1. Foundations of Spirituality

	Rating	Who can help you improve?
Saturation in Scripture		
Spiritual disciplines		
Holy Spirit sensitivity		

Take a few minutes to reflect on what you personally learned from this mission assignment.

Love People

Strengthening Your Chemistry

> *Affection is responsible for nine-tenths of*
> *whatever solid and durable happiness*
> *there is in our natural lives.*
>
> **C. S. Lewis**

CHEMISTRY FOCUSES ON LOVING PEOPLE WITH ALL YOUR SOUL.

◆ The core emphasis of chemistry is summed up in the second part of the Great Commandment, "Love your neighbor as yourself."

◆ Chemistry is shown to us in the relationships that Jesus had with the people around him.

◆ You will grow in chemistry as you begin to understand God's great love for people and let that love grow in your heart.

Prayer

Lord, create in me a heart to love people. Help me to see in every person the image of God. Fill my heart with love for the last, the lost and the least. Give me spiritual eyes, so that I can minister to their deepest needs.

Leaders who are strongest in chemistry are created by God to love people. They know how to create an inviting and contagious atmosphere of love and joy that permeates personal relationships both inside and outside their church or Christian organization. They are designed by God to communicate the importance of living in the realm of the soul.

Chemistry gifts are shown to us in the relationships Jesus had with his disciples, followers and the people he encountered in towns and villages. People grow in chemistry as they experience God's great love for people and let that love grow stronger in their heart.

Those with the chemistry gift focus on the who and when. Who am I to connect with, and when can I do that? Chemistry people are often the ones who invite you into Christian fellowship and make you want to stay. They create a warm environment in which you will feel cared for, encouraged and nurtured. People who are strongest in chemistry are always thinking about how they can make a stronger relational connection. When chemistry leaders build upon spirituality, they encourage others to nurture their relationships with both God and other people. Chemistry people foster authentic and loving relationships with other people, helping them feel accepted, loved, satisfied and whole. Relationships are the context in which spiritual growth most often occurs. As we live life together in Christian community, we learn to live 1 Corinthians 13—to be loving, trusting, hopeful, perseverant, patient, kind and humble.

Chemistry people experience joy and fruitfulness when they do the following:

- show love
- spread joy
- hug
- practice hospitality
- care for people
- encourage
- recruit
- party

◆ welcome

◆ celebrate

◆ live with enthusiasm

◆ love the stranger

◆ model the fruits of the Spirit

In Rodney Stark's book *The Rise of Christianity*, he reports that a major factor in the remarkable growth of Christianity in the Roman Empire was the way in which Christians demonstrated selfless love to people, particularly in times of plague and famine. Christians were willing to risk their very lives and give up their possessions to care for the sick and dying.[1] For chemistry people, loving others is never a means to an end but is the end in itself. Chemistry people can be extravagant lovers: they will invite you into their home, give you food and drink, and welcome you as if you were a family member.

Often, spirituality or strategy people do not understand how critically important and helpful chemistry people are to the life of a church or Christian organization. In a very real sense, chemistry people embody the soul of Christianity. Love is the central value in Christianity, and chemistry people are best at expressing love. They provide the relational glue that holds the body together. Employing their love and connectional gifts, they play a major role in attracting and retaining new people for a church or organization. As Dr. Martin Luther King Jr. said, "Love is a potent instrument for social and collective transformation."[2]

THE THREE CORE FOUNDATIONS OF CHEMISTRY

The three core foundations of chemistry are interpersonal chemistry, team chemistry and crowd chemistry. In order to grow stronger in chemistry, it is necessary to invest a significant amount of time and energy strengthening each core foundation.

God created people to interact in three spheres of social relationships. The first sphere is the interpersonal, in which an intimate connection occurs between two or three people. The second sphere is that of team or group, which ranges in size from five to seventeen people. The third sphere is that of the crowd, which begins from about seventy people and can reach sizes of up to ten thousand persons or even more. There are different social and spiritual needs that can be met in each of these spheres, and each requires its own particular leadership methods and practices. In addition, God works in each of those spheres to produce a different type of spiritual fruit.

Interpersonal chemistry. It is amazing that in both the Old and New Testament God communicated his message in a way that was appropriate for the size of each group. God employed interpersonal chemistry as he spoke to Adam and Eve, Moses, David and Esther in an intimate manner. He spoke in this same way to Jesus at his baptism and to Paul on the road to Damascus. The God of the universe is a personal God and he communicates with us in very personal ways. Blogger Peter Lawler writes,

> The focus on a salvation that depends on faith and not works is . . . one that's kept the focus on the particular connection between the personal creature and the personal Savior, and so it is an antidote to the kind of self-obsession that comes with believing that one's fate is solely in one's hands. It is also an antidote to materialistic self-obsession, of course, in emphasizing that the key personal quality is personal love—or the virtue of charity.[3]

There is a special power in intimate communication, which is why strengthening interpersonal communication skills is so critical for a Christian leader.

Interpersonal chemistry helps us know that we are not just one of the crowd or even just one of a team, but that we are each individuals who God cares about with a tender and personal love. We can in response extend that same kind of love to each individual we know or meet.

Team chemistry. The second social setting in the Bible involves the sphere of the team or group. It is significant that in the Old Testament there were twelve patriarchs and in the New Testament there were twelve disciples, since eight to twelve is an optimal size for a team.

People have an innate need to be part of a middle-sized group where they can know others and be known by them. Team leadership and communication requires a different skill set than when communicating to an individual and can be more challenging. In a team setting, the leader has to be aware of and watch for the interactions of all the members of the team so that a healthy family system can develop.

One of the very first ministry activities of Jesus was to call to himself a team that he would work with, shape and mold. The twelve disciples were a motley, complex group. They spoke the same language and shared many cultural similarities but were also very different in personality and perspective. Three were identified by Jesus as the internal team leaders—Peter, John and James. Others developed a specific identity and role—Thomas became the contrarian; Judas became the treasurer and traitor. James and John were given a special nickname: the "Sons of Thunder." I am sure they created some explosive incidents during their travels. Andrew was the winsome evangelist.

Why did Jesus choose to work with a team? Jesus was interested in forming them spiritually, relationally and missionally, and knew that the team dynamic of this size of a group would play a very important role in shaping the heart, soul and mind of each disciple. Chemistry people are gifted in leading teams like this because they know how to love each person deeply and how to help each person connect with the whole group. Martin Luther King Jr. said, "Hold regular retreats with no more than twelve people in a place that is conducive to deep thinking and serious discussion."[4] Ruth Haley Barton says that

> the purpose of journeying together in spiritual friendship and spiritual community (whether there are just two of you or whether you are in a small group) is to listen to one another's desire for God, to nurture that desire in each other and to support one another in seeking a way of life that is consistent with that desire.[5]

Teams in a church or organization have great transformative power for each participant, because the group dynamic can create a spiritual, social and task dimension that can lead to increased maturity.

Team chemistry involves creating an environment in which the members of the group are transformed by the spiritual engagement, relational dynamics and ministry activities of the team.

Crowd chemistry. The third avenue in which the chemistry gift can be used is the crowd. Jesus had an amazing ability to draw crowds. In the Gospel of Mark, after Jesus called his team of twelve disciples, he immediately began his ministry by going to a synagogue and teaching. Then James and John went with Jesus to Peter and Andrew's house, where the mother-in-law of Peter had a fever. Jesus healed her, causing the whole town to gather at the door (see Mk 1:33). The Gospels relate that Jesus drew away and then fed a crowd of over five thousand people. Throughout the ministry of Jesus, the crowds kept coming and played an important role in each twist and turn of the Gospel drama.

There is a spiritual power attached to each group size; God does a different work in the lives of the people in each of these settings. Through crowd chemistry, people are highly motivated to join a group and willing to commit themselves to the mission and goal of the group. Most people enjoy being part of a crowd where they experience the energy, cohesion and excitement that occurs in large group settings. I will never forget the 163rd game of the 2009 Minnesota Twins season. When the 162-game season ended, Detroit and Minnesota were tied and needed to play a sudden-death game to determine who would advance to the playoffs. My son and I were at that game, in what was then the noisiest stadium in all of baseball, the Minneapolis Metrodome. With every play, the crowd responded in unison, whether the roar of elation or the groan of despair. The energy and excitement was incredible! This was our team, and we were caught up with the rest of the crowd in cheering our team on, contributing enthusiasm and energy to help our team win. It was a thrilling game, with the Twins winning the four-and-a-half-hour game in the twelfth inning, 7 to 6 over the Tigers. I convey my deepest condolences to all Tigers fans.

In a church setting, Christians are encouraged by the solidarity of the crowd. It is a powerful reinforcement of their commitment as followers of Jesus. It is also a safe place for seekers where they can "hide" as they explore Jesus. Crowd leadership and communication requires a different set of skills than communication to an individual or a team, and it can be much more challenging. In a crowd setting, leaders have to watch, and be aware of, the large group energy and dynamic, so they can lead and guide the crowd to coalesce around a set of mutually owned ideals, values and goals.

Crowd chemistry gifts help a Christian leader read and understand the crowd dynamic. God can use the unique qualities of this social setting to produce a lasting impact in each person's life through his or her experience of the crowd's spiritual intensity, its cohesive dynamics and its culture-changing ministry impact.

Few Christian leaders understand crowd chemistry better than Billy Graham. When Shelly and I lived in California in the 1990s, our family participated in two different Billy Graham crusades, in Oakland and in Sacramento. Both as volunteers and as part of the crowd, we were caught up in an incredibly moving experience. We heard inspiring music, followed by Graham's clear gospel presentation. We were astonished at the sight of literally thousands of people getting to their feet and responding to Dr. Graham's simple invitation. For us, the Holy Spirit's presence was palpable. Shelly vividly remembers working at a book table where she handed out the book *Your New Life in Christ* to those who had just made a faith commitment. She was very moved when an elderly man came to her table and asked for the book, saying that he had just given his life to Jesus. Even though he was old and near the end of his time on earth, a brand new life had just begun for him. He was newly born, just a babe in Christ. The crowd context has a special power to help an individual experience the essence of the Christian faith. In this case, it was the context in which God did a mighty, life-changing work in the seekers' hearts and encouraged and emboldened the faith of the believers who witnessed it.

THE CHEMISTRY EXAMEN

Spend some time slowly reading through this chemistry examen and answer the questions placed before you.

Today, I commit myself to loving people with all my soul by growing in the three components of chemistry.

Opening prayer. Lord, create in me a heart that loves people. Help me to see every person as made in your image. Fill me with love in my heart for the last, the lost and the least. Give me spiritual eyes so that I can minister to their deepest needs.

Am I growing in love in my interpersonal relationships?

♦ Am I letting God fill me with love, joy, peace, patience, kindness, goodness faithfulness, gentleness and self-control?

♦ Am I showing those fruits of the Spirit to those around me?

♦ Am I listening carefully to each person by intentionally asking them questions and encouraging them?

Am I growing both in love and in leadership ability with the groups and teams I work with?

♦ Am I blessing them, by modeling interpersonal relationships that are honest, open, encouraging and connecting?

♦ Am I creating teams that both include and embrace people?

♦ Am I balancing our team activities by setting aside time for

• growing in our spirituality?

• developing better group chemistry?

• planning for the mission of God we have been given?

• learning to become better leaders?

Am I growing in my leadership ability and love for the crowd?

♦ Am I growing in my ability to observe large gatherings and understand what is needed to help the crowd experience a more engaging and inclusive atmosphere?

♦ Am I learning how to increase a large group's energy, connection and unity?

◆ Am I improving my communication by listening to other excellent sermons and talks?

◆ Am I evaluating my own sermons and talks, and receiving wise listener feedback, so that I become a better communicator?

Concluding prayer. Thank you, O God. Fill me with love for the people you have brought into my life. Help me hear the Spirit's leading in how I can be a good friend to them. Help me love my relatives, friends, neighbors, people at my church and work, and those in my life who do not know Jesus. Amen.

MISSION ASSIGNMENT—THE THREE FOUNDATIONS OF CHEMISTRY

Rate yourself in the three foundations of chemistry, giving a 1 to the foundation you consider your strongest, a 2 to the intermediate foundation and a 3 to the weakest foundation. Then write down the name of a Christian leader you personally know who has been a role model for you of strength in each foundation.

Table 7.1. Foundations of Chemistry

	Rating	Who can help you improve?
Interpersonal chemistry		
Team chemistry		
Crowd chemistry		

What did you learn from this exercise?

8

Love the World

Strengthening Your Strategy

> *Transmit it logically by confronting reality,*
> *formulating strategy, accepting responsibility,*
> *celebrating victory and learning from defeat.*
>
> **John Maxwell**

STRATEGY FOCUSES ON LOVING THE MISSION OF GOD WITH ALL YOUR MIND.

- The core emphasis of strategy is summed up in the Great Commission.

- Strategy is demonstrated to us in the mission Jesus had toward the world, especially toward the lost and hurting.

- You grow in strategy as you experience God's love for the world, and translate that love into physical acts of mission and service.

Prayer

Lord, create in me a passion and desire for the mission of God in the world. Daily remind me of your great love for all people, love so great that you sent your son Jesus as the sacrifice for the sins of the world. I offer myself as a sacrifice to labor in the mission of God in the world.

Leaders who are strongest in strategy have a strong instinct to love the world by fulfilling the mission of God in the world. They know how to develop a series of sequential actions that will produce fruitful ministry in line with God-directed goals. They demonstrate their love for the world through working with others to create and organize life-changing

ministries in their church, community and world. They are designed by
God to create a "can-do" missional atmosphere through entrepreneurial
imagination. They minister primarily through the realm of the mind.

Strategy finds its foundation in the Great Commission: "Therefore
go and make disciples of all nations, baptizing them in the name of
the Father and of the Son and of the Holy Spirit, and teaching them to
obey everything I have commanded you. And surely I am with you
always, to the very end of the age" (Mt 28:19-20).

The strategy gift is demonstrated in Jesus' mission, especially
toward the lost and hurting. You will grow in strategy as you experience God's great love for the world and translate that love into
physical acts of mission and service.

Strategy is how the good news becomes active and physical in our
world. It especially uses the mind, hands and feet to incarnate the
gospel with real people in real places. Strategy focuses on the questions *how* and *where*. How can we implement and expand the mission
of God? Where are we to do this?

Strategy utilizes the gospel of Jesus Christ (spirituality) and the relational abilities of his disciples (chemistry) to help followers of Jesus live
out the mission of God in the world. Strategy turns ministry ideas into
physical plans and actions. It is an organized method that brings about
growth in Christ's kingdom. Strategy people are fruitful, productive,
efficient, visionary, faith filled, mission oriented, motivated, purposeful,
plan oriented and catalytic. They like to create vision, goals, structures
and organization, and they are known for their hard work, energy and
focus. They like to plan the timetable, organize the people, create the
structure and procure the finances necessary to reach their goal.

Strategy people experience joy and fruitfulness when they do the
following:

◆ plan

◆ organize

◆ strategize

◆ envision

- delegate
- administrate
- sequence
- create efficiency
- develop sustainability
- start new ministries
- reinvent outdated ministries
- transition unfruitful ministries
- safeguard financial integrity
- create financial strength
- train workers

The words and activities of Jesus set the pattern for our mission. Jesus had five central messages that correlate with his five missions. These create a framework that allows the gospel story to be more fully integrated into your life and the life of your church or organization.

The Gospels frequently refer to Jesus as a prophet. In the Old Testament tradition of prophet, Jesus' use of symbolic actions was perhaps even more important than his use of words. As a prophet, Jesus lived out each of his five messages through his day-to-day ministry and accomplished his mission through five decisive eternal actions. Jesus had clarity regarding his message, and he intently and resolutely proceeded to act out that message in dramatic fashion—on the cross, in the grave, through the resurrection, at the ascension and on the day of Pentecost. Chapters 11 through 16 in my book *The American Church in Crisis* describe in detail why the message and mission of Jesus are required to present the whole gospel.[1]

JESUS' MESSAGE

Here are the five messages of Jesus that he declared through his words:

1. He came to forgive our sins and reconcile us with God.
2. He came to destroy the power of Satan and deliver people from bondage.

3. He came to change hearts of stone to hearts of flesh.

4. He came to treat people with compassion, mercy and justice, as God's loved creation.

5. He came to invite and summon followers to become the new people of God.

JESUS' MISSION

While words told the message of Jesus, his actions communicated his mission. Each mission is the physical expression of the corresponding message and allows the message to become even more powerful as it is physically demonstrated.

1. Jesus would be the sacrifice for the sins of the whole world, by dying on the cross.

2. Jesus would fight the decisive battle with Satan, triumphing through the grave.

3. Jesus would be authenticated as the Son of God through the resurrection.

4. Jesus would challenge earthly principalities and powers through his ascension.

5. Jesus would establish his church as the new people of God through the day of Pentecost.

Every Christian is called to learn, embody, tell and incarnate the story of Jesus. We do this personally, integrating it into our lives and expressing it through our words and deeds. We also do it communally as the message and mission of Jesus is implemented in our churches and Christian organizations.

The first message and mission of the church. The church is to proclaim the message of forgiveness in Christ, which leads to reconciliation with God. This is called *evangelism.* It happens publicly and personally when people are both loved by and confronted with Jesus— his message and mission.

The second message and mission of the church. The church is to help people break the bonds that hold and oppress them, helping restore in them God's original creation. This is called *ministry*. It happens through prayer, healing and practical help that leads to a restored image of God. **The third message and mission of the church.** The church is to help people live a new, resurrected life in Christ through the filling and empowerment of the Holy Spirit. This is called *discipleship*. It happens through teaching, Bible study, discipleship, spiritual disciplines and mentoring.

The fourth message and mission of the church. The church is to be a countercultural force in the community, nation and world. This is called *love*. It happens locally, regionally and globally through compassion, mercy, justice and righteousness.

The fifth message and mission of the church. The church is to be God's community of broken yet healing people that provides love, support and accountability for each other. This is called *true community*. It happens through love, worship, fellowship, feasting and communion, and it multiplies through church planting.

THE THREE CORE FOUNDATIONS OF STRATEGY

A critical role for Christian leaders is to implement the message and mission of Jesus in their church or organization. Strategy is required for its implementation, and this is done through focusing on the three core foundations of strategy: envisioning, building and managing. In order to grow deeper in strategy, it is necessary to invest a significant amount of time and energy strengthening each core foundation.

Envisioning. The first core foundation is envisioning. Envisioning occurs when a leader perceives and discerns the structures and organizations that God wants to create for the future, so that the future can be fruitful. One of the greatest Christian vision casters was Dr. Martin Luther King Jr. The following are some of his quotes about the importance and power of a vision:

> The movement is led as much by the idea that symbolizes it. The role of the leader is to guide and give direction and philosophical under-building to the movement.

Call your vision a dream. It will be more meaningful, more simplistic, and more symbolic.

Make sure your dream taps into the emotion of people.

Tell the people that you either go up together, or you go down together.

Your organization will prosper or die as a result of your ability to create, embody, and communicate a vision.[2]

Vision helps others to visualize God's preferred future. Vision is the picture of how the message and mission of Jesus will be communicated and lived out to your neighbors, community, culture and world. This vision needs to capture the imagination of people. It needs to help them see the possibilities in being involved in a great endeavor that will make a significant difference for the kingdom of God.

Building. The second core foundation is building. Building occurs when a leader creates a step-by-step process to construct ministries that will fulfill the vision, while enlisting other leaders to become colaborers in that building process. The primary structures and organizations that need to be brought into being should be based on the message and mission of the church. They should answer these five questions:

◆ How will we see people come to faith in Christ?

◆ How will the gospel set people free from the things that hold them in bondage?

◆ How will people's hearts be transformed, and how will they grow deeper as disciples?

◆ How will the last, the lost and the least be helped through ministries of compassion, mercy and justice?

◆ How do we create a new community, made up of followers of Jesus, that loves, grows and serves?

Jesus incarnated the mission of God in our world, and the church is meant to continue that mission.

Managing. The third core foundation is managing. Managing occurs when a leader implements and executes the ministry plans that produce fruit year after year. This is done through organization, delegation, management and administration. In the Gospels, Jesus gives us many examples of how he managed those he worked with. Consider how he trained the Twelve, selected an inner circle of leaders (his leadership team) and delegated the preparations for the Passover meal. Consider the detailed instructions that he gave the seventy-two in Luke 10. Jesus advised them on when they should enter a town, where they should stay, what not to bring and what to say, so that they could minister wisely and fruitfully when proclaiming the gospel and healing people.

THE STRATEGY EXAMEN

Spend some time slowly reading through this strategy examen and answer the questions placed before you.

Today, I commit myself to loving the mission of God with all my mind, by growing in the three components of strategy.

Opening prayer. Lord, create in me a passion and desire for the mission of God in the world. Daily remind me of your great love for all people, a love so great that you sent your son, Jesus, as the sacrifice for the sins of the world. I offer myself as a sacrifice, to labor in the mission of God in the world.

Am I growing in love for the mission of God by growing stronger in my ability to envision?

♦ Am I seeking a vision from God regarding what needs to be created to fulfill God's mission?

♦ Am I providing, along with other leaders, direction and vision for the mission of God in our church or organization?

♦ Am I striving to continually make this vision simple, clear, concrete and compelling?

♦ Does this vision connect spiritually, emotionally and intellectually with people?

♦ Is this vision shaping the culture of our church or organization?

Am I growing in love for the mission of God by growing stronger in my ability to build fruitful structures?

◆ Am I learning how to create a step-by-step process to build ministries that will be fruitful?

◆ Am I enlisting other leaders that can be part of the building process?

Am I growing in love for the mission of God by growing stronger in my ability to manage?

◆ Am I becoming stronger in organizational skills?

◆ Am I becoming stronger in delegation?

◆ Am I becoming stronger in training leaders and workers?

◆ Am I becoming stronger in administration?

Concluding prayer. Thank you, O God. Help me turn my aspirations into physical ministry progress. Help me make and deepen disciples, show compassion and justice to the last and the least, and advance the kingdom of God on this earth. Amen.

MISSION ASSIGNMENT—THE THREE FOUNDATIONS OF STRATEGY

Rate yourself in the three foundations of strategy, giving a 1 to the foundation you consider your strongest, a 2 to the intermediate foundation and a 3 to the weakest foundation. Then write down the name of a Christian leader you personally know who has been a role model for you of strength in each foundation.

Table 8.1. Foundations of Strategy

	Rating	Who can help you improve?
Envisioning		
Building		
Managing		

What did you learn from this exercise?

9

Love Wisdom

Strengthening Your Leadership

> *The single biggest way to impact an organization is to focus on leadership development. There is almost no limit to the potential of an organization that recruits good people, raises them up as leaders and continually develops them.*
>
> **John Maxwell**

LEADERSHIP WISDOM FOCUSES ON FOLLOWING THE LEADERSHIP EXAMPLE OF JESUS WITH ALL YOUR STRENGTH.

♦ The core emphasis of leadership wisdom is summed up in Paul's leadership principle, "Follow my example, as I follow the example of Christ" (1 Cor 11:1).

♦ Leadership wisdom is demonstrated to us in how Jesus led his disciples.

♦ Christian leaders grow in leadership wisdom as they answer Jesus' prayer that "your kingdom come, your will be done" (Mt 6:10) and let that desire grow in their hearts.

Prayer

Lord, help me to become a stronger and wiser leader. Help me to watch and follow the example of Jesus, observing how he led with great wisdom. Help me to learn from the numerous Scriptures that talk about the blessedness of wisdom. May this wisdom from God become instrumental in developing people and make a difference in changing our world.

The presence of spirituality, chemistry and strategy does not automatically produce a good leader. After all, by themselves, three individual legs are not enough to make a stool. There is another component, the seat of the three-legged stool. The seat keeps all three legs firmly anchored and provides the structure that completes and makes the stool useful. In the same way, the seat of leadership wisdom, supported by strong legs of spirituality, chemistry and strategy, helps leaders to grow in leadership capability so that they can respond wisely in every ministry situation they encounter. Leadership wisdom produces leadership presence, which followers see when a leader is filled with godliness, knowledge, wisdom, humility, strength, confidence, power, love and the Holy Spirit.

In both the Old Testament and New Testament, wisdom is perhaps the most important factor for living and leading a godly life. It is mentioned 215 times in the book of Proverbs alone. The New Testament presents Jesus himself as the personification of wisdom. A simple definition of wisdom is seeing God's perspective on a situation and knowing how to respond based on the wisest choice.

In the secular world, the word *wisdom* is seldom associated with leadership. But for Christian leaders, wisdom is the preeminent attribute of leadership. When Christian leaders use leadership wisdom to teach, mentor, model, focus, clarify and encourage, those they lead will be filled with wisdom, fruitfulness and joy, and will produce a multiplied harvest.

THE THREE CORE FOUNDATIONS OF LEADERSHIP WISDOM

The three core foundations of leadership wisdom are leader instinct, leader fruitfulness and leader multiplication. In order to grow deeper in leadership wisdom, it is necessary to invest a significant amount of time and energy strengthening each core foundation.

Leader instinct. The first core foundation is leader instinct, which is formed when experience is shaped by wisdom, allowing the leader to intuitively grasp key leadership challenges.

In the biological world, *instinct* is defined as "a largely inheritable and unalterable tendency of an organism to make a complex and specific response to environmental stimuli without involving reason."[1] In this definition, instinct is viewed as an inborn, unchangeable quality. An additional definition from *Merriam-Webster's Collegiate Dictionary* that fits human experience better is "a natural or inherent aptitude, impulse, or capacity <had an *instinct* for the right word>."[2] When a person has an "instinct for the right word," it was not hardwired into the person from birth but was developed as he or she learned a language, read widely and understood the meaning and function of particular words. We will use the word *instinct* in this section to refer to unconscious thoughts or actions that are conditioned into a person through repetitive behaviors, habits or experiences.

The best coaches in sports prize instinct in their top recruits. Instincts are honed in athletes when they practice a particular move so many times that it becomes second nature for them. When they are in a game situation, they just know what to do without having to think or reflect.

Christian leaders likewise becomes wiser and stronger as they develop sound instincts. Leader instincts are formed when leaders process and reflect on their experiences through the lens of wisdom, to understand what happened and how God was at work in that situation. This accumulation of wisdom will begin to allow the leader to instinctually know what to do and say and how to act in a particular situation. This is why the combination of experience and wisdom is so crucial for Christian leaders. God created your brain so that you can see patterns and then apply wisdom to your response in each situation.

Leader fruitfulness. The second core foundation is leader fruitfulness, which describes how a leader helps the church or Christian organization focus on producing fruit that lasts.

We have a large apple tree beside our house, and I am amazed at the number of luscious apples that are waiting to be picked in the next few weeks. I watch in awe the process of development from bud, to flower, to fruitlet, to a mature apple that is bursting with flavor. In Christian leadership, it is the fruit that counts. *Spiritual fruit is produced when human activity is touched by the Holy Spirit.* Spiritual fruit is germinated by the actions of faithful Christians, who attempt to live out the instructions of Scripture in harmony with the Holy Spirit. While activity has a critical role in initiating the fruit-producing process, human activity alone can never bring about the miracle that is seen in the production of fruit. When God takes the human activities of believers and divinely touches their effort, lasting fruit is produced. Wise leaders learn to pray for, look for and measure fruitfulness, rather than just focusing on the activity.

In the last few years many Christian leaders have begun to introduce new measurements to determine the productivity and fruitfulness of their organizations or churches. They once only counted the number of members, the amount of money collected and the attendance at certain events. Today leaders are elevating the value of fruitfulness by measuring with different standards, such as changed lives, sacrificial living and dedicated discipleship. A new set of metrics are being utilized to more accurately evaluate how God is producing fruit in the harvest field.

Leader multiplication. The third core foundation of leadership wisdom, multiplication, occurs when Christian leaders prioritize leading other leaders rather than only leading the crowd. This is done through modeling, mentoring and mobilizing. Jesus is the model for how we are to develop leaders. His plan was shown in the calling of the twelve disciples. They had an intensive three-year immersion experience by traveling with Jesus, watching him minister, listening to his teaching and preaching, gaining frontline ministry experience, observing the challenges and threats that came with frontline ministry and engaging in the spiritual practices of Jesus.

Every year I spend four to five days with a cohort of leader friends on a retreat. All are younger than I am. We share, encourage, challenge, eat, play, explore and talk from dawn to bedtime. It is the most encouraging, ruthlessly honest and spiritually enriching time I experience all year long. A few years ago, our cohort met in Encinitas, California. One of the members of the group invited the retired senior pastor of a large church to be our guest one afternoon. We had two hours to ply him with questions and soak up his leadership wisdom. Here was the most important statement he made to us: "I used to think my staff members were the critical people I needed to invest in. The longer I was there, the more I realized that staff would come and go, but lay leaders would stay. I discovered that they were the most important people to the long-term health and growth of our church."

I suggest mentoring three or four leaders each year whom you can invest time in, who will travel with you to appointments and events and who will gather with you for focused retreats. This will let you observe their current habits and challenges, mobilize them for ministry and create a team that will encourage each other in what God might do through them.

THE LEADERSHIP EXAMEN

Spend some time slowly reading through this leadership wisdom examen and answer the questions placed before you.

Today I commit myself to loving and leading like Jesus loved and led, with wisdom and with all of my strength, by growing in the three core foundations of leadership wisdom.

Opening prayer. Lord, help me to become a stronger and wiser leader. Help me to watch and follow the example of Jesus, observing how he led with great wisdom. Help me to learn from the Scriptures that talk about the blessedness of wisdom. May this wisdom come from God, become instrumental in developing people and help to change our world.

Am I growing stronger and wiser in leader instincts?

◆ Am I consistently evaluating the ministry experiences I have and using wisdom to learn lessons on how to grow as a leader?

◆ Am I learning from other leaders' experiences and wisdom so that I can incorporate those learnings as my own?

◆ Am I talking through my leadership experiences with other leaders, asking them what suggestions and advice they might give me to help me become a stronger leader?

Am I growing stronger and wiser in leader fruitfulness?

◆ Am I measuring God's transformation in the people I lead?

◆ Am I honestly assessing the real changes brought about in our community and world by our church or organization?

◆ Am I working with other leaders and coaches to expand our ministry fruit for Christ?

◆ Is this focus on fruit changing the culture of our church or organization?

Am I growing stronger and wiser in leader multiplication?

◆ Am I prioritizing leading other leaders rather than just leading the crowd?

◆ Am I multiplying leaders through modeling the development of other leaders?

◆ Am I multiplying leaders through personally mentoring a group of leaders?

◆ Am I multiplying leaders through mobilizing others to invest in leaders?

Concluding prayer. Thank you, O God. Fill me with the wisdom necessary to lead in a godly manner. Teach me to lead with personal integrity in all areas of my life by treating all people well and by helping the people of God start a revolution that turns this world upside down. Amen.

MISSION ASSIGNMENT—THE THREE FOUNDATIONS OF LEADERSHIP WISDOM

Rate yourself in the three foundations of leadership wisdom, giving a 1 to the foundation you consider your strongest, a 2 to the intermediate foundation and a 3 to the weakest foundation. Then write down the name of a Christian leader you personally know who has been a role model for you of strength in each foundation.

Table 9.1. Foundations of Leadership Wisdom

	Rating	Who can help you improve?
Leader instinct		
Leader fruitfulness		
Leader multiplication		

What did you learn from this exercise?

The three legs and the seat of the Leadership Stool each have three core foundations. Each triad is composed of the three most important areas for skill development in that area to help the leader grow stronger in spirituality, chemistry, strategy and leadership wisdom.

◆ The core foundations of spirituality are saturation in Scripture, spiritual disciplines and Holy Spirit sensitivity.

◆ The core foundations of chemistry are interpersonal chemistry, team chemistry and crowd chemistry.

◆ The core foundations of strategy are envisioning, building and managing.

◆ The core foundations of leadership wisdom are leader instinct, leader fruitfulness and leader multiplication.

I recently led a seminar with an ethnically diverse group of twenty-five Christian leaders using this tool. Like you will do shortly, they ranked themselves on the twelve core foundations, beginning with their strongest and ending with their weakest. The top four are a person's gift areas. I invited individuals in the group to stand up and share with each other their top four. Ten volunteered. Because everyone knew each other, there were lots of head nods, smiles, affirmations and even amens. Each person received the genuine affirmation of God's gifts to them from the group.

As I ranked myself along with the group, I was somewhat surprised by which one came out first. Even though I was very familiar with the exercise, it helped me see in a new light how God has used some of my gifts in ministry. I hope you will be enlightened and surprised when you take this simple inventory.

These twelve core foundations are displayed in the Leadership Wheel diagram.

Rate yourself in these twelve foundations of Christian leadership, giving a 1 to the foundation you consider your strongest and continuing until you identify the weakest foundation with a 12. I've found it's easiest to begin by rating your top four in order, then selecting your lowest four, and finally sequencing the middle four.

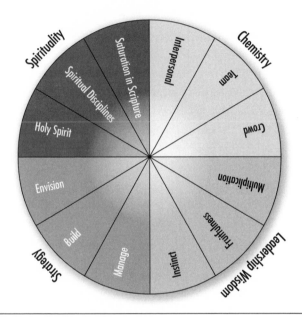

Figure 9.1. The leadership wheel

The website offers an online inventory that will evaluate you in the twelve core foundations and produce a customized growth plan and accompanying resources to strategically strengthen your core foundations, based on your responses in the online inventory. It is called the "Personal Growth Tool" and is found at sixstyles.org/growthtool.php. There is a nominal charge for this growth tool.

THE SIX LEADERSHIP STYLES

Section Three is the heart of the book. This section will lead you into a much deeper understanding of how God created you to lead and serve. The sequence of your three legs determines which of the six styles of leadership is yours. Each of the six styles represents a unique set of gifts that allows everyone with that style to minister in a similar manner for Christ. Each style is described in detail to help you understand who you are, how you were designed to minister, what fruit will be produced by your style and what are some of the potential pitfalls.

10

The Six Styles

There are different kinds of gifts, but the same Spirit distributes them. There are different kinds of service, but the same Lord. There are different kinds of working, but in all of them and in everyone it is the same God at work. Now to each one the manifestation of the Spirit is given for the common good.

1 Corinthians 12:4-7

So far, you have learned about how spirituality, chemistry, strategy and leadership wisdom work together to provide a conceptual and practical paradigm for leading. This will enable you to observe people and structures with fresh insight and clarity. This third section will show you an even more important discovery: identifying your Christian leadership style.

In Romans 12:6, 1 Corinthians 12:4-7 and elsewhere, Paul teaches that God has given different types of gifts to Christians. While there is unity in the body of Christ, there definitely is not uniformity. Instead, the diversity that Scripture celebrates in God's whole creation is also reflected in the gifts of Christians.

Four years ago I was flying from Minneapolis to Los Angeles. I had been using the three-legged leadership model as a teaching instrument for two or three years. As I settled into my seat, a thought came into my mind. *If there are only three legs, there can only be six possible sequences of the combination spirituality, chemistry and strategy.* I wondered to myself, *Can I name those six? Will people lead in a manner similar to others with their style?* By the time the plane landed, I had named the six styles and was eager to find out whether each group was distinct from the other five in its leadership style.

The Leadership Stool model identifies six distinct Christian leadership styles. The sequence of the scores of your strongest, intermediate and weakest legs indicate which leadership style God has given you. Leaders who are strongest in chemistry are either inspirational leaders or relational leaders. Leaders who are strongest in spirituality are either imaginative leaders or sacred leaders. Leaders who are strongest in strategy are either building leaders or mission leaders.

All six styles have equal value in the body of Christ. Each style brings together a unique set of leadership gifts and perspectives that help build God's kingdom, with each style contributing something that the other five do not. When all six styles work together, they demonstrate the completeness and unity of the body of Christ while affirming the variety of personalities and gifts given by the Holy Spirit. Most important, each of the six styles employs a different way of leading.

Growing in your leadership style requires an understanding of the role of your strongest leg, of how the intermediate leg can magnify the fruit of your strongest leg, and of specific ways to bolster your weakest leg. The results and fruit of your ministry will differ significantly from someone with a different leadership style. When you read your style report, you may be surprised at how accurately it describes you. As you learn about your unique style, you will gain insight into how God created you, showing you a clear pathway to become a stronger and wiser leader. As you read about the other five styles, the descriptions will give you insights into how God created others you know and work with and why they lead as they do.

THE SIX LEADERSHIP STYLES

✝ *1. Sacred leaders.* Sacred leaders are strongest in spirituality, intermediate in chemistry and weakest in strategy. They are gifted by

God to connect spiritually with people and encourage them to grow deeper in their knowledge and relationship with God, while paying close attention to the voice of the Holy Spirit. Sacred leaders are spiritually sensitive people. An adjective often used to describe the role of a sacred leader is *deep*. They lead through their ability to genuinely connect with people by communicating the deep things of God. Many sacred leaders have the Ephesians 4:11 gift of teacher. Mary (the sister of Martha), John and Isaiah are three biblical examples of sacred leaders.

2. Relational leaders. Relational leaders are strongest in chemistry, intermediate in spirituality and weakest in strategy. They are gifted by God to emotionally connect with individuals and groups, and to inspire them to follow Jesus and love each other. An adjective often used to describe relational leaders is *loving*. They naturally lead through their ability to create caring relationships with large numbers of people. Many relational leaders have the Ephesians 4:11 gift of pastor or shepherd. Barnabas, Esther and Philip are three biblical examples of relational leaders.

3. Inspirational leaders. Inspirational leaders are strongest in chemistry, intermediate in strategy and weakest in spirituality. They are gifted by God to connect powerfully with a crowd and motivate them to follow Jesus by engaging in the mission of God. An adjective often used to describe inspirational leaders is *motivational*—they lead through their ability to inspire and influence people, especially through public speaking. Inspirational leaders excel at getting people to rally around a vision. Many inspirational leaders have the Ephesians 4:11 gift of evangelist. Peter, Joshua and Elijah are three biblical examples of inspirational leaders.

4. Building leaders. Building leaders are strongest in strategy, intermediate in chemistry and weakest in spirituality. They are gifted by God to strategize for growth and enlist others to help enlarge the mission of God. They are best described as knowing how to grow organizations. They instinctively know how to create the right conditions and systems that produce numeric growth and stronger ministry so that more people will come, join and serve. Most building leaders have a growth gift and an organizational gift. They have a hybrid Ephesians 4:11 gift that I call an "apostolist"— having some of the qualities of an apostle and some of the qualities of an evangelist. Deborah, Nehemiah and Joseph are three biblical examples of building leaders.

↑ 5. Mission leaders. Mission leaders are strongest in strategy, intermediate in spirituality and weakest in chemistry. They are gifted by God with the spiritual vision needed for the immediate future. They call people to follow a deeper gospel and then multiply new expressions of the mission of God. A word often used to describe a mission leader is *multiplier.* Mission leaders call people to live out an active gospel while multiplying disciples, programs and ventures. Their best fruitfulness comes through reproducing new leaders, new ministries and new churches. Many mission leaders have the Ephesians 4:11 gift of an apostle. Paul, Gideon and Moses are biblical examples of mission leaders.

☀ 6. Imaginative leaders. Imaginative leaders are strongest in spirituality, intermediate in strategy and weakest in chemistry. They are gifted by God to receive a vision from God for this generation and motivate people to step out in faith and live out a new way of being the people of God within their culture. An adjective often used to describe an imaginative leader is *creative.* They use their spiritual creativity to synthesize new models and then use strategy to implement those imaginative ideas. Many inspirational leaders have the Ephesians 4:11 gift of a prophet. Samuel, Daniel and John the Baptist are biblical examples of imaginative leaders.

Understanding and valuing all six styles will help you avoid two common pitfalls. First, most people overvalue their own style and undervalue styles that are different from their own. For example, sacred leaders seldom resonate with inspirational or building leaders.

The opposite is also true. The beauty of the diversity of gifts and styles is tarnished when a Christian leader believes his or her style is the most valuable one and implicitly diminishes the importance of the other five styles.

CHALLENGES FOR EACH STYLE

A second pitfall is an inordinate focus on the deficiencies of the other styles. This can be avoided by understanding that every style has specific weaknesses. The following are challenge areas for each of the leadership styles.

1. *Sacred leader.* A common challenge of sacred leaders is their lack of *practical usefulness.* They often struggle to translate their deep spirituality into physical ministry productivity.

2. *Relational leader.* A common challenge of relational leaders is their lack of *clear focus.* They love being with people but often do not know where or how they should lead those people.

3. *Inspirational leader.* A common challenge of inspirational leaders is their lack of *deep foundations.* Often they are so busy spending time with groups or crowds that they do not take enough time to break away and nurture scriptural depth or intimacy with God.

4. *Building leader.* A common challenge of building leaders is their lack of *vital spirituality.* Managing the expanding fruit of their ministry usually consumes so much of their time and energy that they have little time left for a strong walk with God.

5. *Mission leader.* A common challenge of mission leaders is their lack of *people sensitivity.* Their strong task orientation and their continual creation of new mission endeavors often keeps them from empathizing with the people they lead.

6. *Imaginative leader.* A common challenge of imaginative leaders is their lack of *relational wisdom.* Their heads can be in the clouds, filled with great ideas, so they often miss critical relational clues sent by those they work with and minister to.

COMPLEMENTARY STYLES

Because people differ in their gifts, passions, personalities and habits, they minister in profoundly different ways. In the circular arrangement of the six leadership styles, individual leaders will find that they are most comfortable with their own style but can expand their leadership effectiveness by learning how to use their complementary style. A person's complementary style can become as strong as their primary style if they learn specific habits that will strengthen their intermediate leg. This is much easier than strengthening their weakest leg and is possible for most leaders through focused attention. Leaders will dramatically increase their leadership influence when they can use both styles to lead.

Here are the complementary styles:

◆ relational leader and sacred leader

◆ inspirational leader and building leader

◆ imaginative leader and mission leader

When sacred leaders learn to also lead as relational leaders, they will significantly increase their leadership ability.

When relational leaders learn to also lead as sacred leaders, they will significantly increase their leadership ability.

When inspirational leaders learn to also lead as building leaders, they will significantly increase their leadership ability.

When building leaders learn to also lead as inspirational leaders, they will significantly increase their leadership ability.

When mission leaders learn to also lead as imaginative leaders, they will significantly increase their leadership ability.

When imaginative leaders learn to also lead as mission leaders, they will significantly increase their leadership ability.

The percentage of leaders who fall into each of the six styles are almost perfectly balanced, as the chart below shows.

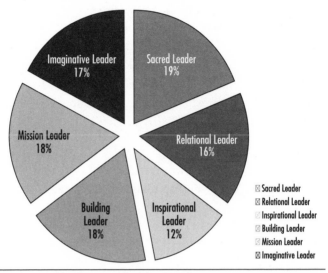

Figure 10.1. Percentage of leaders in each of the six styles

It is also instructive to look at the differences in the leadership styles of males and females. In four styles, the percentages are quite similar, with the exception of the building leader, which has twice as many males, and the relational leader, which has almost twice as many females.

Table 10.1. The Percentage of Females and Males in the Six Christian Leadership Styles

	Female	Male
Sacred leader	21%	19%
Relational leader	21%	13%
Inspirational leader	11%	12%
Building leader	11%	21%
Mission leader	19%	17%
Imaginative leader	17%	17%

The next six chapters will paint a picture of the beautiful diversity of each of the six Christian leadership styles. While you will be most interested in your own style, appreciate the symphony created by all six styles, as it will help you understand and appreciate each style God has created.

MISSION ASSIGNMENT—DIVERSITY IN STYLE

When I put the numbers in my database and discovered that each style except inspirational leaders contained almost an identical percentage of people who fit into that category, I was shocked! Statistics never work out that evenly.

1. Do you have any idea why the five styles came out with virtually the same percentage?

2. Do have any idea why inspirational leaders had a lower percentage?

11

✝ The Sacred Leader

Always remember that only if one builds, as Saint Paul says, on the foundation which is Jesus Christ, will one be able to construct something really great and lasting. . . . Walk towards Christ. He alone is the solution to all your problems. He alone is the way, the truth, and the life; He alone is the real salvation of the world; He alone is the hope of mankind.

Pope John Paul II

Sacred leaders have an amazing gift of helping people experience the depths of God himself.
Sacred leaders are strongest in spirituality, intermediate in chemistry and weakest in strategy. Sacred leaders are spiritually sensitive. They encourage others to pay attention to the voice of the Holy Spirit and to grow closer in relationship to God. They lead through their ability to genuinely connect with people through the communication of the deep things of God. A verb to describe their role is *deepen*. Many sacred leaders have the Ephesians 4:11 gift of teacher.

Biblical examples of sacred leaders are Mary, the sister of Martha; John, the disciple; and Isaiah. Luke 10 tells us that Martha was upset that Mary "sat at the Lord's feet listening to what he said" (Lk 10:39). "'Martha, Martha,' the Lord answered, 'you are worried and upset about many things, but few things are needed—or indeed only one. Mary has chosen what is better, and it will not be taken away from her'" (Lk 10:41-43). Mary desired above all else to have an intimate relationship with

Jesus, sit in his presence and learn from him. Sacred leaders will benefit from studying the lives of these three biblical characters to better understand the character, behavior and style of sacred leaders. Howard Thurman, J. R. R. Tolkien, Dallas Willard, Ruth Graham Bell, Dietrich Bonhoeffer, Richard Foster, Oswald Chambers, Pope John Paul II, St. Francis of Assisi and Beth Moore are historic and contemporary examples of sacred leaders. Reading their biographies and writings will give you new insights into how God can use sacred leaders. What leaders do you know personally who are sacred leaders? A term that describes the role of the sacred lay leader is *God focuser*. They are called to encourage others to keep their eyes fixed on Jesus, encouraging and exhorting others to go deeper and further in their knowledge and experience of God.

Sacred leaders will recognize many of the following characteristics in themselves: they are devout, Spirit minded, God loving, God fearing, reverent, virtuous, pure of heart, Christlike, peace loving, deep, reflective, contemplative, insightful, earnest and meditative.

Three friends stand out among the many who have been influential sacred leaders in my life. One has been a good friend and mentor to me over the last twenty years, and for the first six of those years was my immediate superior. He has an uncanny ability to see beyond outward appearances and perceive the true underlying causes. So many times when I talked with him, it seemed that God had given him direct revelation into some of the challenges I was facing. He combined this unusual discernment with a listening ear, spiritual wisdom, wise questions and a heart of compassion.

Another friend tests out as a sacred leader, although his spirituality percentage is only slightly higher than his chemistry score. Most people would guess that his strongest leg is chemistry—people first notice John's warm and caring connection with them as individuals. The gift and discipline that makes him a sacred leader is his intense focus on studying Scripture. He has been highly influenced by his seminary professor and leadership expert Bobby Clinton, who taught him to engage in very detailed studies of specific books of the Bible, where he'd often

spend three years in an in-depth study of a particular book.
Another sacred leader is Shelly, my wife. When it comes to reading people, especially the motivations of their hearts and the purity of their intentions, she is very gifted. Her perceptions, both spiritually and relationally, are almost always spot on, and that wisdom has helped me avoid many missteps.

God has created sacred leaders with a unique way of leading. They have gifts specific to their specific leadership style that are not natural strengths for other styles. By recognizing how they are gifted to lead, they will more readily understand their role in the kingdom of God. Understanding their profile will help them know how they can be most effective as leaders in God's vineyard and more confident and aware of how God can use them to produce lasting fruit.

USING THEIR STRONGEST LEG, SPIRITUALITY

Sacred leaders' strongest leg, spirituality, is the area of their greatest ministry fruitfulness. It is a God-given gift. Because this area comes naturally to them and brings them joy, they prefer to spend most of their ministry time using their spirituality gift. Unfortunately, this will limit their influence for Christ. They should enjoy and maximize their spirituality gift but become adept at using both chemistry and strategy to augment their spirituality.

Sacred leaders' best gift to others, the church and the world is to live for God and develop a close relationship with God. They can discern spiritual things and the movements of the Spirit. Because they are sensitive to the inner world of people, they understand the intrapersonal (what occurs within a person) and are aware of people's thoughts, feelings and especially motivations.

Sacred leaders can be gifted writers and accomplished public speakers. Although they procrastinate and experience anxiety as they write articles or craft talks, they are insightful, creative, deep and thoughtful. They are confident their message is from God and can write and speak with spiritual authority. Sacred leaders may hear a word from God for another person and can help that person discern God's will and direction for themselves. Each of the six styles has a special type of intelligence. Sacred leaders have gifts in intrapersonal intelligence, which is the ability to know what is occurring within a person. Most sacred leaders have had an attraction to God since they were young. An important role of a sacred leader is to help people experience how to live in the realm of the Spirit. A teachable and self-aware sacred leader is most significantly used by God when he or she lives a life saturated in Scripture, practices spiritual disciplines daily and lives in dependence on the voice and movement of the Holy Spirit.

DEVELOPING THEIR INTERMEDIATE LEG, CHEMISTRY

Sacred leaders' intermediate leg, chemistry, is their secret weapon. Their chemistry leg will enable them to spread the influence of their strength in spirituality by using their relational abilities to help individuals foster a life of spiritual depth and authenticity. Their intermediate leg, chemistry, is always easier to develop than their weakest leg, strategy, because they are naturally stronger in that leg and have a better intuitive grasp of how to use it. For sacred leaders, the most effective ways to use their chemistry to lead people into a deeper spirituality are through mentoring individuals, facilitating small groups and public speaking opportunities.

Most sacred leaders are good at one-on-one chemistry. They are aware of and sensitive to how the other person feels. They offer their undivided attention, causing that person to feel truly listened to, cared for and understood. Sacred leaders have valuable insights to offer in a group but need time to form their thoughts and the boldness to share them. Sacred leaders understand people internally but need to improve their understanding of how people interact with each other socially.

DEVELOPING THEIR WEAKEST LEG, STRATEGY

Sacred leaders' weakest leg, strategy, has the potential to sabotage otherwise good ministry or possibly get them fired. To develop in this area, most sacred leaders will need a respected mentor or strategy coach who can give them wise counsel and offer accountability in their development. For most sacred leaders, strategy can feel unnatural and uncomfortable.

A sacred leader's potential to become a stronger leader depends on both growing in understanding of strategy and wisely using strategy people. Weakness in this area will significantly diminish their fruitfulness. Special attention needs to be given to translating their deep spirituality into physical ministry. Wise sacred leaders surround themselves with trusted mentors and leaders who are strong in strategy. Sacred leaders need coworkers who are adept at understanding and implementing strategy to create forward momentum for the organization. In addition, creating a strategy team in their church or organization will expand its strategic thinking.

By nature and habit, sacred leaders can spend 60 to 70 percent of their time using their strongest leg, spirituality, 20 to 35 percent using their intermediate leg, chemistry, and only 5 to 10 percent using their strategy leg. A more balanced approach would be a 50 to 30 to 20 ratio. Their time allocation can improve by being aware of their use of time and by spending more time on chemistry and strategy. They will benefit from studying the lives of biblical characters who were strong in spirituality and who also used wise strategy to maximize their spirituality gift.

THE SHADOW SIDE OF SACRED LEADERS

The shadow side of sacred leaders is three potential challenges they can face: spiritual pride, oversensitivity and excessive self-criticism. Spiritual pride occurs when a person considers himself or herself to be more insightful than other Christians. Sacred leaders are often overly sensitive to criticism and can be overly critical of themselves. They set high personal standards and can experience excessive guilt and self-condemnation when they fall short of the ideal. Sacred leaders can also react negatively to correction or criticism from others.

Sacred leaders are inward-focused and may not be aware of the people and environment around them. They can be so focused on their own thoughts and feelings that they don't perceive how others are experiencing them. If they do not intentionally ask questions—a persistent challenge for most sacred leaders—they can be unaware of the opinions or thoughts of others.

Each of the six Christian leadership styles has two deep needs common to that style. These needs are deeply rooted within them, and the leader is often unaware of them. Each of these hidden needs can have a positive side but also a more profound dark side. Sacred leaders have a *deep need for affirmation*. Most people do not recognize or fulfill this inner need. Sacred leaders need to receive specific words of encouragement but need to reciprocate by giving encouragement to others. They also have a *deep need to be right*. They are often right because of their gifts of wisdom and discernment, but they may ignore or diminish other opinions and thoughts.

THE TEN COMMANDMENTS FOR SACRED LEADERS

1. Realize that most of your ministry fruit will come from your spirituality gift. Focus on using these gifts in harmony with the promptings of the Holy Spirit. Be bold!

2. Keep reminding yourself of the need to produce tangible products and results.

3. Push yourself to write every day, whether journaling or writing an article.

4. If your chemistry score is low (under 50%), you will be helped by talking to a wise chemistry leader about how to improve in relational skills and habits.

5. Sacred leaders often make good spiritual directors. Many Christian colleges and seminaries offer courses, certificates and degrees in spiritual direction. Sacred leaders find this a great choice for a continuing education program.

6. Remember to exercise the gift of faith in God's ability to use you. You have a strong belief in God. Believe as strongly in God's ability to use you!

7. Sacred leaders can easily become isolated from people. You need friends with whom you consistently have meaningful conversations.

8. Physical exercise, interaction with beauty and fun activities are vital sources for your replenishment.

9. Pay attention to your physical, financial, emotional and relational well-being.

10. The complementary style for a sacred leader is the relational leader. If you work at intentionally strengthening your chemistry, this will give you a second powerful leadership style to use in ministry.

LIFE SCRIPTURE FOR THE SACRED LEADER

Be strong and very courageous. Be careful to obey all the law my servant Moses gave you; do not turn from it to the right or to the left, that you may be successful wherever you go. Keep this Book of the Law always on your lips; meditate on it day and night, so that you may be careful to do everything written in it. Then you will be prosperous and successful. Have I not commanded you? Be strong and courageous. Do not be afraid; do not be discouraged, for the LORD your God will be with you wherever you go. (Josh 1:7-9)

MISSION ASSIGNMENT—REFLECTING ON SACRED LEADERS

1. Describe a specific situation where a sacred leader used his or her spirituality gift to help you become strong in your faith. What was that leader's lasting influence in your life?

2. Pick one of the biblical characters referenced in this chapter who was a sacred leader. Describe how this individual was most powerfully used by God.

3. Who do you know personally who might be a sacred leader? Have that person read this chapter, and ask him or her whether this description is accurate.

12

💬 The Relational Leader

More than anything else today, followers believe they are part of a system, a process that lacks heart. If there is one thing a leader can do to connect with followers at a human, or better still a spiritual level, it is to become engaged with them fully, to share experiences and emotions, and to set aside the processes of leadership we have learned by rote.

Lance Secretan

Relational leaders have an amazing gift of helping people and groups experience love in a real and personal way.

Relational leaders are strongest in chemistry, intermediate in spirituality and weakest in strategy. A verb to describe their role is *love*. They are gifted by God to connect emotionally with individuals and inspire them as a group to follow Jesus and love each other. They naturally lead through their ability to create caring relationships with large numbers of people. Many relational leaders have the Ephesians 4:11 gift of pastor or shepherd.

Biblical examples of relational leaders are Barnabas, Esther and Philip. Did you know Barnabas's real name was Joseph? A companion of Paul, his relational gift was so powerful that he was renamed Barnabas, which meant the son of encouragement. We first hear about Barnabas when he sold a field he owned and generously gave the proceeds to the church. He was happy to share what he had with others. He also offered emotional and ministry support to Paul and his companions. Relational leaders will benefit from studying the lives of these three biblical characters to better understand the character, behavior and style of relational leaders. Can you think of other biblical characters who might be relational leaders?

Jim Rayburn, Doug Coe, Efrem Smith, Garth Bolinder and Lloyd John Ogilvie are historic and contemporary examples of relational leaders. Reading their biographies and writings will give you new insights into how God can use you as a relational leader. What leaders do you know personally who have been relational leaders? How have you been influenced by them?

Relational leaders will recognize the following characteristics in themselves: they hearten, assure, cheer, invigorate, urge, exhort, stir up, give hope, boost, champion, sustain, support and advocate.

A term that describes the role of a relational lay leader is *people encourager*. They are gifted at connecting with individuals and engaging with them emotionally. People encouragers create an atmosphere of love and joy in a group.

Another friend has been both my pastor and a good friend. He tests strongest in chemistry but is also strong in spirituality, in part because of the tradition of black preaching and spirituality that his African-American background has taught him. He uses his chemistry gifts to make the scriptural message attractive, engaging and exciting as he lays down a strong fabric of spirituality in each sermon. This motivates and encourages the listeners to desire to live a life following God.

As far as I can tell, another friend of mine has over five hundred Christian leader friends throughout the world. He is on the boards of Bible Study Fellowship International and Gordon-Conwell Theological Seminary. His genius is his ability to give individual attention to people. He loves people and is able to authentically make a person feel like he or she is one of the most important persons in the whole world at that particular moment. He also makes sure that he regularly follows up and maintains the connection with those friends.

God has created relational leaders with a unique way of leading. They have gifts specific to their own leadership style that are not natural strengths for other styles. By recognizing how they are gifted to lead, they will more readily understand their role in the kingdom of God. Understanding their style will help them to be more effective as leaders in God's vineyard and more confident of how God can use them to produce lasting fruit.

USING THEIR STRONGEST LEG, CHEMISTRY

Their strongest leg, chemistry, is the area of their greatest ministry fruitfulness. It is a God-given gift. Because this area comes naturally to them and brings them joy, they often like to spend most of their time using their chemistry gift. The chemistry gift provides more immediate, emotional rewards than does either spirituality or strategy. These rewards can become like a drug for relational leaders, and the desire to interact with people can become addictive. Relational leaders love the positive emotion, energy and attention they receive from people—but they can also spend so much time and energy loving and caring for people that they do not develop their spirituality or strategy legs. Unfortunately this will limit their influence for Christ. They should enjoy and maximize their chemistry gift but become adept at using the other two legs too.

Relational leaders use their chemistry gift to create unity and love in a group. They pay close attention to people's reactions and know how to keep them engaged through emotional investment. When in a group, relational leaders like to play, eat, talk, love, laugh, care, relate and unite. They genuinely consider the welfare of the other person. An important role of relational leaders is to model the fruits of the Spirit in their relationships and ministry. They are particularly gifted at spreading love and joy.

Relational leaders are often drawn toward people-helping ministries such as counseling, visitation and pastoral care. Relational leaders can also be great networkers. As an example, they would be wise to use their networking gifts to bring in outside leaders to teach their people about growth in specific areas of spirituality or to teach their teams how to more effectively use strategy. Relational leaders have interpersonal intelligence, which is the ability to understand relationship dynamics between individuals. Relational leaders typically live on a rather practical level in their communication to people, wanting to make sure that the gospel makes sense in their everyday lives.

Churches led by relational leaders often grow quickly at first because of their personal attractional abilities, but that growth can flatten out or even decline as the group reaches the sociological limit on their size. Without the development of spirituality and strategy, relational leaders will have a difficult time providing a whole and satisfying church experience over an extended period of time.

Relational leaders often have good emotional intelligence, but they sometimes misread people and situations. They can believe that everyone thinks, feels and acts just as they do. Growth in spiritual and strategic intelligence will help bring balance to their emotional intelligence.

DEVELOPING THEIR INTERMEDIATE LEG, SPIRITUALITY

Relational leaders' intermediate leg, spirituality, is their secret weapon. Their spirituality leg will give depth to their strength in chemistry because they will use spiritual depth to help others foster a life of spiritual vitality and authenticity. Their intermediate leg, spirituality, is easier to develop than their weakest leg, strategy, because they are naturally stronger in that leg and have a better intuitive grasp of how to use it. They can usually develop and execute a growth plan for themselves in spirituality. Their weakest leg, though, usually requires a consistent connection with a coach or mentor to keep them on track and accountable. Using spirituality to develop greater biblical depth in their preaching and teaching is a key way for relational leaders to become stronger.

Relational leaders use their intermediate leg, spirituality, to show Christians how to love each other and how to live together in harmony. Their spirituality, grounded in Scripture that instructs them to express their faith in acts of love and mercy, helps them to focus on those in need—especially the last, the least and the lost. This often becomes an important part of their church's missional focus. Relational leaders passionately want the lives of Christians to be grounded in love for God, love for each other and love for their community. Continued growth in spirituality is critical for maximizing their ministry. Relational leaders have the ability to be strong in spirituality when they strengthen their habits of Scripture study and develop a deeper, more consistent devotional life. Relational leaders can be effective preachers but often do not spend enough time in the biblical study and sermon preparation that are needed to present excellent messages week after week. In many cases, relational leaders' sermons are liked but over time do not provide their congregations with enough substance and new spiritual insight. Sometimes relational leaders hear the complaint that no matter which text they speak on, their sermons make the same point week after week. Developing their complementary style, the sacred leader, will help them to become better speakers.

Art Greco, a close pastor friend and relational leader, offered the following when I asked him for advice for relational preachers:

> Sermons are a channel for your relational ability, allowing people to emotionally connect with the Scripture. The spirituality side has to be tenaciously sought. I feed on a regular diet of listening to good preachers and reading biographies of great preachers. To get material for my sermons, I spend time reading, watching movies, listening to music, enjoying relationships and keeping up on the news. Part of your motivation to be a strong preacher has to flow out of your deep love for people and the congregation. Even the power of the need for affirmation can help motivate relational leaders to improve their sermons. In a sermon, I help people feel deeply about their relationship with God. In prayer, I picture people and possibilities and use these pictures in my sermons.

DEVELOPING THEIR WEAKEST LEG, STRATEGY

The relational leader's weakest leg, strategy, has the potential to sabotage otherwise good ministry or possibly get the leader fired. Most often, it is the weakest leg that creates frustration with a leader's performance and fruitfulness. To develop in this area, relational leaders will need a respected mentor or coach who can offer wise counsel and accountability.

Relational leaders need to give special attention to developing a clear focus. They love being with people but often do not know where or how they should lead those people. Regularly strategizing with a team composed of trusted strategy people will help relational leaders immensely. It is important for them to consider the three components of strategy—envisioning, building and managing—when developing a personal growth plan for their weakest leg. Envisioning answers the questions *why* or *what*, and provides clarity and goals for the next phase, building, which answers the questions *where, when* or *how*, and results in stronger ministry organizational structures. Managing will allow what is built to have ministry fruitfulness year after year.

Relational leaders always learn best in groups. Learning by themselves or in a crowd is not nearly as helpful. Wise relational leaders will schedule their personal development plan within the context of their preferred group dynamic. Art Greco offers the following suggestion for senior pastors:

> If you are in a larger church, it is important for relational leaders to build a strong staff. One of the challenges facing most relational leaders is they don't like to share recognition with others. Hire who you relate well with, but make sure they have different strengths from yours. Hire based on style as well as on adaptability.

By nature and habit, relational leaders typically spend 70 to 75 percent of their time using their chemistry leg, 20 to 25 percent using their spirituality leg and only 5 to 10 percent using their strategy leg. A more balanced approach would be a 50 to 30 to 20 ratio. This can improve by spending more time cultivating better habits in spirituality and strategy. For example, as you read your daily Scripture passage, use a commentary to understand its deep meaning. Ask yourself each evening what specific ministry goals were accomplished today.

THE SHADOW SIDE OF RELATIONAL LEADERS

Each of the six Christian leadership styles has two deep needs that are inherent to it. These needs are deeply rooted within them, and the leader is usually unaware of them. Each of these hidden needs can benefit the leader, but they can also have a more profound dark side. Relational leaders have a *deep need for attention*. They want to be liked, want to be in the limelight and have a need to please people—this is what causes them to be adept at human relationships, but the deep need for attention can be very self-focused. They also have a *deep need for affirmation*. They are very good at giving encouragement but need a lot of encouragement in return.

THE TEN COMMANDMENTS FOR RELATIONAL LEADERS

1. Develop better self-awareness by asking trusted friends incisive questions about yourself.

2. Get leadership advice from wise leaders who are not directly in ministry.

3. Find a ministry colleague who is a building leader. Ask that person to mentor and coach you in organizational leadership.

4. Initiate friendships with mission leaders and utilize their gifts of foresight and planning.

5. You will best develop spirituality and strategy in the company of others. For example, form a Scripture study group with colleagues. Learn to plan out details of strategy and organization when you are physically present with others. Follow this rule, and you will become much more productive.

6. Find a preaching coach, especially one who can help you preach with biblical depth.

7. Be careful not to become a people-a-holic. Keep a proper balance of enjoying social environments while maintaining adequate time alone and with your family.

8. Use creative methods of Scripture study in order to keep your biblical knowledge fresh and growing. There are many great technology tools available to assist you.

9. Spend time on Monday organizing your week, scheduling necessary time for leading other leaders, preparing sermons and performing administrative tasks. Schedule a planning retreat with other leaders twice a year.

10. The complementary style for a relational leader is the sacred leader. If you increase your knowledge and time investment in spirituality, this will give you a second powerful leadership style for use in ministry.

LIFE SCRIPTURE FOR THE RELATIONAL LEADER

Dear friends, let us love one another, for love comes from God. Everyone who loves has been born of God and knows God. Whoever does not love does not know God, because God is love. This is how God showed his love among us: He sent his one and only Son into the world that we might live through him. This is love: not that we loved God, but that he loved us and sent his Son as an atoning sacrifice for our sins. Dear friends, since God so loved us, we also ought to love one another. No one has ever seen God; but if we love one another, God lives in us and his love is made complete in us. (1 Jn 4:7-12)

MISSION ASSIGNMENT — REFLECTING ON RELATIONAL LEADERS

1. Describe a specific situation where a relational leader used his or her chemistry gift to love you and make you feel important. What was the lasting influence in your life?

2. Pick one of the biblical characters referenced in this chapter who were relational leaders. Describe how the person was used most powerfully by God.

3. Who do you know personally who might be a relational leader? Have the person read this chapter, and ask him or her whether the description is accurate.

13

✻ The Inspirational Leader

Leadership is not so much about technique and methods as it is about opening the heart. Leadership is about inspiration—of oneself and of others. Great leadership is about human experiences, not processes. Leadership is not a formula or a program; it is a human activity that comes from the heart and considers the hearts of others. It is an attitude, not a routine.

Lance Secretan

Inspirational leaders have an amazing gift of motivating both Christians and seekers to desire a stronger connection with Jesus and join together to positively change society.
Inspirational leaders are strongest in chemistry, intermediate in strategy and weakest in spirituality. They are especially gifted by God to connect with a crowd and inspire them to follow Jesus. The result is that the group is inspired to engage in the mission of God, from their own back yard to the very ends of the earth. A verb to describe their role is *motivate*—they influence people, especially through public speaking. Inspirational leaders excel at catalyzing people to rally around a vision. Many inspirational leaders have the Ephesians 4:11 gift of an evangelist.

Peter, Joshua and Elijah are biblical examples of inspirational leaders. Both Peter and Elijah were involved in large crowd events, where their preaching brought about radical change in their listeners. Elijah preached in the presence of 450 prophets of Baal, but his sermon was meant for another group. According to the British prince of preachers,

Charles Spurgeon, "The vast mass of that day belonged to a third class—they were those who had not fully determined whether fully to worship Jehovah, the God of their fathers, or Baal, the god of Jezebel."[1] It was to them that the inspirational leader Elijah delivered his sermon, calling on them to abandon Baal and follow the God of Israel. Inspirational leaders will benefit from studying the lives of these three biblical characters to better understand the character, behavior and style of inspirational leaders. Can you think of any other biblical personalities who might be inspirational leaders?

George Whitefield, Danny DeLeon, John Maxwell, Aimee Semple McPherson, Robert Schuller, Luis Palau, Craig Groeschel and Billy Graham are historic and contemporary examples of inspirational leaders. Reading their biographies and writings will give you new insights into how God can use you as an inspirational leader. What leaders do you know personally who are inspirational leaders? How have you been influenced by them?

A term that describes the role of an inspirational lay leader is the *group mobilizer*. These leaders are gifted in connecting with a group or a crowd and can motivate as well as mobilize people, so that productive ministry is accomplished in the world.

Inspirational leaders will associate many of the following verbs with themselves: they enliven, invigorate, motivate, inspire, vitalize, activate, spark, spur, impel, rouse, awaken and kindle.

I have four friends who exemplify the traits of an inspirational leader. The first's greatest gift is understanding crowd chemistry, but he is also very good at team chemistry. He likes being in the center of the action. He likes challenging those who are far from God to come to Jesus. He has always had a very strong inborn desire to do evangelism, in great measure because he did not grow up in a Christian family. He has the exceptional ability to invite unbelievers to life in Christ in a compelling and culturally appropriate way. He is insistent to make sure that each person who responds gets proper follow-up, care and nurture in their new faith so that they will grow in Christ and become enfolded into the church.

Another friend was a church planter whom I worked with twenty years ago and who is now the pastor of the largest church in America. The church has an incredible influence throughout the world. He has a strong gift of an evangelist—Billy Graham is his hero. One of the reasons for the church's amazing growth is that he wisely hired three very capable senior leaders early in the life of the church, each of whom had strong gifts in areas different from his own.

Another friend is a gifted evangelist who loves being in front of a crowd. He is an incredible optimist and always believes the best in people and expects the best out of God. A final friend is an inspirational leader who is ever-smiling, always positive and continually seeking the person who is far from God. He can always sense how to best talk about spiritual things to a person in a way that will attract them to God.

God has created inspirational leaders with a unique way of leading. They have gifts specific to their own leadership style that are not natural strengths for other styles. By recognizing how they are gifted to lead, they will more readily understand their role in the kingdom of God. Understanding their style will help them to be more effective as leaders in God's vineyard and more confident and aware of how God can use them to produce lasting fruit.

USING THEIR STRONGEST LEG, CHEMISTRY

Their strongest leg, chemistry, is the area of their greatest ministry fruitfulness. It is a God-given gift. Because this area comes naturally to them and brings them joy, they want to spend most of their ministry time using their chemistry gift. Unfortunately, this will limit their influence for Christ. Inspirational leaders should enjoy and maximize their chemistry gift but become adept at using the other two legs.

Inspirational leaders use their chemistry gift to create ownership and momentum in a group. They pay close attention to the reactions of both individuals and the entire group, and they know how to keep people mentally and emotionally engaged. Inspirational leaders can often lead in a way that results in the rapid numeric growth of their church or organization. Their challenge is to encourage spiritual and structural depth that is commensurate with that growth. If the church gets larger without its base becoming wider and deeper in spirituality and strategy, the church will lack stability.

Inspirational leaders often have the gift of an evangelist. They intuitively know how to engage people in conversations about God and can do it in a winsome way that encourages further relationship and dialogue. Inspirational leaders usually have social intelligence and intuitively understand the relational dynamics of a group or crowd.

The gift of an evangelist is a critical gift for the church today, as fruitful evangelism is becoming more challenging as the culture changes. Inspirational leaders should discern how and when to use this gift and how to maximize it. They should make sure their church or organization has created strong and reliable systems for the follow-up and assimilation of new believers, to help root them in their faith. They should not neglect this gift—they should fan it into flame and create a structure and process for evangelism to happen naturally in their church or organization.

For inspirational leaders, an important component of their ministry fruitfulness is their ability to promote. However, overpromising can be a part of promoting. Some people will view them as shallow unless they display a commensurate depth of character and humility.

DEVELOPING THEIR INTERMEDIATE LEG, STRATEGY

Inspirational leaders' intermediate leg, strategy, is their secret weapon. It enhances and maximizes the potential of their strongest leg. Their strategy leg assists by helping the leaders implement their strong chemistry instincts in ways that produce real, physical ministry and helpful organizational structures. The intermediate leg is always easier to develop than the weakest leg. People are naturally stronger in their intermediate leg and have a better intuitive grasp of how to use it. Growth in envisioning, building and managing is the most effective way for inspirational leaders to become better leaders.

Inspirational leaders use strategy to create ministry programs and momentum in their church and community. Their strategy gifts help them envision and build ministries that advance God's kingdom. They are highly motivated to create events and programs where people become followers of Jesus and grow deeper in Christ. Continued growth in strategy is critical for maximizing ministry. Inspirational leaders are especially gifted in creating a focus on a specific, compelling theme, planning the sequential development of the activity, team involvement and event planning.

DEVELOPING THEIR WEAKEST LEG, SPIRITUALITY

Inspirational leaders' weakest leg, spirituality, has the potential to sabotage otherwise good ministry or possibly get them fired. It is usually this weakest leg that causes frustration with the leaders' performance. To develop in this area, they need a respected mentor who can give them wise counsel and provide accountability.

The most common areas in which inspirational leaders need to grow are maintaining consistent practices of Bible study and regularly spending time alone with God. Their potential to become stronger leaders will depend on growing in spirituality, as ignoring this will significantly diminish their potential. The primary reason for this weakness is that inspirational leaders spend so much time focusing on their public ministry that they do not take the time to personally pursue greater scriptural depth or intimacy with God. It would be helpful for them to build close relationships with respected Christian leaders who are strongest in spirituality, who can help them grow deeper in fellowship with God. It is important to consider the three components of spirituality when developing a growth plan—saturation in Scripture, spiritual disciplines and Holy Spirit sensitivity.

By nature and habit, inspirational leaders can spend 60 to 65 percent of their time using their chemistry leg, 25 to 30 percent using their strategy leg, and only 10 to 15 percent using their spirituality leg. A more balanced approach would be a 50 to 30 to 20 ratio. This will change only through an awareness of their time expenditure and a focus on spending more time developing spirituality and strategy.

THE SHADOW SIDE OF INSPIRATIONAL LEADERS

Each of the six Christian leadership styles has two deep needs that are common to that style. These needs are deeply rooted within them, and the leader is usually unaware of them. Each of these hidden needs can have a positive side but also a more profound dark side. Inspirational leaders have a *deep need for attention*. All leaders strongest in chemistry have this need. Inspirational leaders have a need to impress people—as a result, they are often adept at team and crowd connections, which is a benefit. However, this need may be motivated by self-centeredness or insecurity. They must be aware of the potential seduction and guard against it. They also have a *deep need for power*. Inspirational leaders like to have influence. They love control and can exercise inordinate power in a church or organization. Developing the habits of receiving feedback from others, asking good questions and listening carefully to their responses is a powerful antidote to the need for power.

Inspirational leaders often struggle with three specific areas and would benefit by asking themselves the following questions:

♦ Inspirational leaders often feel a strong sense of betrayal when people leave their church or organization. How will they deal with those feelings?

♦ Inspirational leaders may evidence a lack of sensitivity to the voice of the Holy Spirit, who is trying to shape their life and ministry. How will they hear the Holy Spirit's voice?

♦ Inspirational leaders are often not truly accountable to anyone else. This can make them vulnerable to temptation in the areas of power, money or sex. To whom will they be accountable?

THE TEN COMMANDMENTS FOR INSPIRATIONAL LEADERS

1. Develop better self-awareness by asking trusted friends incisive questions about yourself.

2. Get advice from wise leaders outside of your ministry context.

3. Be faithful in taking a day off each week.

4. Develop a friendship with a sacred leader and meet regularly.

5. Take a half-day spiritual retreat once a month.

6. If married, listen to the wisdom of your spouse.

7. Your complementary style is the building leader—by developing stronger strategy gifts, you will be able to use that style with equal ease.

8. Find a trusted spiritual director or mentor to challenge you in biblical and spiritual growth.

9. Be careful not to exaggerate or overpromise.

10. Hold material possessions loosely.

LIFE SCRIPTURE FOR THE INSPIRATIONAL LEADER

Devote yourselves to prayer, being watchful and thankful. And pray for us, too, that God may open a door for our message, so that we may proclaim the mystery of Christ, for which I am in chains. Pray that I may proclaim it clearly, as I should. Be wise in the way you act toward outsiders; make the most of every opportunity. Let your conversation be always full of grace, seasoned with salt, so that you may know how to answer everyone. (Col 4:2-6)

MISSION ASSIGNMENT—REFLECTING ON INSPIRATIONAL LEADERS

1. Describe a specific situation where an inspirational leader used his or her chemistry gift to create a powerful crowd experience with God. How did it make you feel? What was its lasting influence in your life?

2. Pick one of the biblical characters listed above who was an inspirational leader. Describe how the person was most powerfully used by God.

3. Who do you know personally who might be an inspirational leader? Have that person read this chapter, and ask him or her whether the description is accurate.

14

♣ The Building Leader

*The best leaders are determined, bold,
and reject inhibitions imposed by
old traditions and habits.*

Martin Luther King Jr.

*Building leaders have an amazing gift of bringing people together
to achieve physical progress in expanding the kingdom of God on
this earth.*

Building leaders are gifted in helping churches and Christian organizations grow and become organizationally effective and efficient. They are strongest in strategy, intermediate in chemistry and weakest in spirituality. A verb that is most often associated with their role is *grow*. They are gifted by God to strategize for growth, to enlist other leaders and then together to lead the way in enlarging the mission of God. They are talented at growing and expanding organizations. They instinctively know how to create the right conditions and systems that produce numeric growth so that more and more people come and join. Building leaders often have a hybrid of the apostle and evangelist gifts of Ephesians 4:11, so I have coined the word *apostelist* to describe this gift.

Biblical examples of building leaders include Joseph, Deborah and Nehemiah. Joseph was an amazing building leader. At one point he seemed least likely to succeed in all of Egypt, but he eventually became the second in command under Pharaoh. Joseph's organizational acumen was evident in his plan to store the surplus corn during the years of abundant harvest, so the Egyptians would have reserves during the years of famine. Building leaders would do well to study the lives of Joseph, Deborah and Nehemiah to better understand the character, behavior and style of building leaders. Who are other biblical characters who might be building leaders?

Mother Teresa, Bill Bright, Bill Hybels and Dawson Trotman are historic and contemporary examples of building leaders. Reading their biographies and writings will give you new insights into how God can use building leaders. What leaders do you know personally who are building leaders? How have you been influenced by them?

A term that describes the building lay leader is *task accomplisher*. These leaders are called by God to expand the kingdom through organizing and implementing specific tasks that produce "more and better" ministry.

Building leaders will recognize many of the following characteristics in themselves. They are focused, confident, direct, purposeful, convincing, inspiring, good at recruiting, visionary, planning, sequencing, results oriented, high performing, persuasive, goal oriented, driven and energetic.

A good friend of mine is a classic building leader whom I have worked with for twenty-five years. He's very focused and driven to grow and advance the kingdom of God. He is focused on the future and how he can help his local church to grow and expand. His four greatest gifts are attracting high-capacity, growth-oriented lay leaders, growing the church numerically, expanding the larger mission of God and developing building facilities through the generosity of the church's members.

Another good friend is strong in both her strategy and chemistry legs. She's a great example of how chemistry is the secret weapon of a building leader. While her first preference is always strategy, her strategy becomes more powerful through her ability to get people invested in the process. She is the queen of communication, connecting with people over the phone, through emails and in person.

God has created building leaders with a unique way of leading. They have gifts specific to their leadership style that are not natural strengths for other styles. By recognizing how they are gifted to lead, they will more readily understand their role in the kingdom of God. This profile is designed to help them know how they can be most fulfilled as leaders in God's vineyard and more confident and aware of how God can use them to produce lasting fruit.

USING THEIR STRONGEST LEG, STRATEGY

Building leaders' strongest leg, strategy, is the area of their greatest ministry fruitfulness. It is a God-given gift. This area comes naturally to them and brings them joy, so they want to spend most of their time using strategy. Unfortunately, this can limit their influence for Christ. They should enjoy and maximize their strategy gift but become adept at using the other two legs.

Building leaders know how to enlarge a church, organization, ministry or group. They have a green thumb in producing growth in God's kingdom. They hold an advanced degree in growthology! They are focused on *more* and *better* and understand how to use vision, goals, structures, organization, hard work, energy and focus to bring about growth and development.

Building leaders exhibit a high degree of confidence. Sometimes, though, behind this show of confidence lies a fear of failure or an inordinate need to achieve. They primarily use their reason to plan for growth. They like to decide on a solution as quickly as possible. They move rapidly ahead in planning the timetable, selecting the right people, creating the structure and gathering the finances necessary to reach their goal. Building leaders are excellent at envisioning the future and planning the necessary sequential steps needed to complete the task. They have strong skills in building and managing, causing them to function like a ministry CEO.

Building leaders need to constantly move forward, and they expect their people and organizations to do the same. Once something plateaus or begins to decline, they often look for another position at an organization with growth potential. Building leaders possess organizational intelligence, the ability to understand how to structure an organization for efficiency and recruit the right people for specific positions.

Building leaders can appear to use people to accomplish their vision and goals. When a person is no longer useful to their goals, these leaders quickly move on from that relationship. It is important for building leaders to ask themselves these questions: "What motivates me and why?" and "Why am I driven toward accomplishment, and how does that affect my relationships?"

DEVELOPING THEIR INTERMEDIATE LEG, CHEMISTRY

Building leaders' intermediate leg, chemistry, is their secret weapon. Chemistry can enhance and maximize the potential of their strongest leg, strategy. Their chemistry leg assists their strategy leg by helping the leader attain individual and group buy-in, which encourages ownership and momentum. The intermediate leg is always easier to develop than the weakest leg. People are naturally stronger in their intermediate leg and have a better intuitive grasp of how to use it.

Building leaders use their chemistry ability to recruit and motivate the right people for their team. They naturally seek out influencers, achievers and the affluent. Building leaders can be good public communicators and effectively use their chemistry gifts to enhance their speaking. They inspire by casting a vision of what God can do through the group. They are well organized, persuasive and direct. If they can learn to communicate with more emotion and a deeper spirituality, their speaking will have a greater impact. Wise building leaders will develop stronger interpersonal chemistry when they take time to connect with others without watching the clock.

DEVELOPING THEIR WEAKEST LEG, SPIRITUALITY

Building leaders' weakest leg, spirituality, receives the least amount of their attention. The most common liability of building leaders is their lack of consistent practices of personal Bible study and inattention to their devotional life. Their strong task orientation often prevents them from spending time alone with God. As Bill Hybels confesses autobiographically, building leaders are too busy to pray, hence the remedy in the title of his book *Too Busy Not to Pray*.

Building leaders' potential to become more balanced will depend on their growth in spirituality. Ignoring it will significantly diminish their leadership. Their weakest leg has the potential to sabotage otherwise good ministry or possibly get them fired. In most cases, a coach, mentor or accountability group will be very helpful in strengthening their spirituality. It is also important that building leaders invest time in the three core foundations of spirituality: saturation in Scripture, spiritual disciplines and sensitivity to the Holy Spirit.

That fact that building leaders are weakest in spirituality does not mean that they cannot develop strength in this area. Instead, it means that they naturally prefer to use strategy first, then chemistry, and finally spirituality, which receives whatever time is remaining. By nature and habit, building leaders can spend 60 to 65 percent of their time using their strategy leg, 25 to 30 percent using their chemistry leg and only 10 to 15 percent using their spirituality leg. A more balanced approach would be a 50 to 30 to 20 ratio. This will improve only with awareness of their actual time expenditures and a focus on developing simple, consistent habits to exercise their spirituality leg.

THE SHADOW SIDE OF BUILDING LEADERS

The shadow side of building leaders can be an insensitive overemphasis on efficiency. They are accomplishment oriented and usually do not think about how their decisions may affect the lives of other people. They are built for productivity and efficiency. One important area for them to grow in is love for people. As building leaders, they should balance their need for accomplishment and efficiency by showing love for others.

Each of the six Christian leadership styles has two deep needs that are common to that style. These hidden needs are so deeply rooted within them that the leader is often unaware of them. Each of these needs can have a positive aspect but also a more profound dark side. Building leaders have a *deep need to overachieve*. Since they want to accomplish as much as possible for God, they often have a difficult time constructing boundaries between their work life and their personal life. They also have a *deep need for power*. The positive side of having power is the ability to influence people. The negative side is the need for control. Building leaders should be alert to how they use their power by focusing on influence rather than control. The best strategy for moderating the need for power is for the leader to ask discerning and wise questions, seek others' perspectives and then let the group play a role in deciding the outcome.

THE TEN COMMANDMENTS FOR BUILDING LEADERS

1. Develop better self-awareness by asking trusted friends incisive questions about yourself.

2. You are a powerful person. Be aware of that, and learn how to create relationships of equality.

3. Identify a person who is strong in biblical insight and passion. Meet regularly with that individual and learn from him or her.

4. Make sure your team activities include lots of chemistry and fun.

5. Take a half-day spiritual retreat once a month, if possible with other Christian leaders.

6. Find a trusted spiritual director or mentor to meet with regularly.

7. Make sure you take a day off each week, and use all your vacation time. If possible, don't think about your job during these times!

8. Identify a pastor who is strong in devotional practices and spiritual disciplines. Meet with and learn from him or her.

9. Make sure that you maintain strong relationships with your best friends. Regularly having fun with them and praying with them will help to keep your life in balance.

10. The complementary style for a building leader is the inspirational leader. If you raise your understanding and practice of chemistry, this will give you a second powerful leadership style for use in ministry.

LIFE SCRIPTURE FOR THE BUILDING LEADER

For this reason, since the day we heard about you, we have not stopped praying for you. We continually ask God to fill you with the knowledge of his will through all the wisdom and understanding that the Spirit gives, so that you may live a life worthy of the Lord and please him in every way: bearing fruit in every good work, growing in the knowledge of God, being strengthened with all power according to his glorious might so that you may have great endurance and patience, and giving joyful thanks to the Father, who has qualified you to share in the inheritance of his holy people in the kingdom of light. For he has rescued us from the dominion of darkness and brought us into the kingdom of the Son he loves, in whom we have redemption, the forgiveness of sins. (Col 1:9-14)

MISSION ASSIGNMENT — REFLECTING ON BUILDING LEADERS

1. Describe a specific situation where a building leader used his or her strategy gift to expand the mission of God. How did it make you feel? What was its lasting influence in the kingdom of God?

2. Pick one of the biblical characters referenced in this chapter who was a building leader. Describe how the person was most powerfully used by God.

3. Who do you know personally who might be a building leader? Have the individual read this chapter, and ask him or her whether the description is accurate.

15

↑ The Mission Leader

Leaders are pioneers. They are people who venture into unexplored territory. They guide us to new and often unfamiliar destinations. People who take the lead are the foot soldiers in the campaigns for change. . . . The unique reason for having leaders—is to move us forward. Leaders get us going someplace.

James M. Kouzes and Barry Z. Posner

Mission leaders have an amazing gift of helping people see what God could accomplish if they left their safety zone and stepped out in faith on a new venture.

Mission leaders are strongest in strategy, intermediate in spirituality and weakest in chemistry. They are gifted by God with spiritual vision to foresee and then implement what is needed in the future. A verb to describe their role is *multiply*. They call people to follow a deeper gospel, while multiplying disciples, programs and ventures. Their best fruitfulness is expressed through raising up new leaders, new ministries and new churches. Mission leaders often have the Ephesians 4:11 gift of an apostle.

Three biblical examples of mission leaders are Paul, Gideon and Moses. Paul is the mission leader par excellence in Christianity. Paul's strongest leg, strategy, allowed him to be a prime mover in the spread of Christianity throughout most of the Roman empire within his generation. Paul's intermediate leg, spirituality, is shown in his writing contribution to the New Testament, where he reveals his deep and creative understanding of the work of Christ. Paul needed help with his chemistry leg—team chemistry could be challenging for Paul. Mission leaders will benefit from study the lives of these three biblical characters to better understand the character, behavior and style of mission leaders. Can you think of any other biblical characters who might be mission leaders?

John Wesley, Franklin Graham, Henrietta Mears, Rick Warren, Dorothy L. Sayers and Chuck Colson are historic and contemporary examples of mission leaders. Reading their biographies and writings will give new insights into how God can use you as a mission leader. What leaders do you know personally who have been mission leaders? How have you been influenced by them?

A term that describes the role of the mission lay leader is the *fruit producer*. These leaders are quick to see new possibilities for missional engagement and use their activist drive to produce new fruit for God.

Tim is what I call a serial church planter. Tim is vitally interested in starting new churches and raising up the young leaders to be the pastors of those new churches. He planted a church in Southern California in 2003, which has since spawned ten new church plants—four of which are in California and six in Mozambique. Tim also wrote an excellent book to help the younger generation think about how they can live out the gospel, titled *Embodying Our Faith*.[1] Tim's motto is "Multiply, multiply, multiply."

Another gifted mission leader was Henrietta Mears, who left a huge influence on the evangelical church culture in Southern California. She loved starting new ministries. She was very influential in writing Christian curriculum for children and adults and began Gospel Light Publications. She started a camp in the San Bernardino mountains called Forest Home, which has had an amazing influence on successive generations of young Christians, helping them become devoted followers and passionate leaders for Christ. Under her leadership, the Sunday school program of First Presbyterian of Hollywood grew from seven hundred students to over four thousand. Three students whose lives she invested in as leaders were evangelist Billy Graham, Senate chaplain Richard Halverson and Bill Bright, the founder of Campus Crusade for Christ (now Cru). Her actions also reflect the motto, "Multiply, multiply, multiply"!

Mission leaders will recognize many of the following characteristics in themselves: they are commissioned, pioneering, Spirit led, fruitful, productive, efficient, visionary, faith filled, discipling, mission minded, skilled at planning and motivating, purposeful, envisioning, incisive, confident and assured.

God has created mission leaders with a unique way of leading. They have gifts specific to their leadership style that are not natural strengths for other styles. By recognizing how they are gifted to lead, they can more readily understand their role in the kingdom of God. This chapter is designed to help them know how they can find fulfillment as leaders in God's vineyard and become even more confident and aware of how God can use them to produce lasting fruit.

USING THEIR STRONGEST LEG, STRATEGY

Their strongest leg, strategy, is the area of their greatest ministry fruitfulness. It is a God-given gift. Because strategy comes naturally to them and brings them joy, they want to spend most of their ministry time using this leg. Unfortunately, that will limit their influence for Christ. They should enjoy and maximize their strategy gift, but become stronger at spirituality and chemistry.

Mission leaders are motivated to turn ministry ideas into physical plans and action. They can become impatient with too much group processing. They have a penchant for initiation and action. Mission leaders enjoy helping other leaders become more effective in fulfilling the mission of God. They are gifted at creating action plans, removing obstacles and moving forward. They like to focus on the critical issues, and when they have achieved clarity, they want to act quickly.

Mission leaders like to ask the questions *what, when* and *how.* "What should we be doing?" "When can we start?" and "How will we best accomplish the goal?" Their focus is on building God's kingdom. They want to fulfill Jesus' prayer, "Your will be done on earth as it is in heaven" (Mt 6:10). Right now!

Mission leaders like to plan and then activate the plan. They want to create a strategy, whether it is for evangelism, feeding the hungry, training disciples, ending social problems, starting new ministries or planting new churches. Mission leaders like to start ministries that do not exist—new programs, new structures and new initiatives. Efficiency and productivity are two highly important values for a mission leader. They like to use their time well and want to produce tangible results. Mission leaders have strategic intelligence, which is the ability to envision the future and develop new structures and systems so that future fruitfulness will occur. Most mission leaders are strongest at envisioning, good at building and not as strong in managing.

Many mission leaders have the gift of an apostle. God works through them to (1) start new churches in new geographical areas, cultures or people groups; (2) develop new leaders, often from the younger generation; or (3) launch new ministries that meet an unmet need. They should pay attention to how God may want to use them in one of these three ways.

DEVELOPING THEIR INTERMEDIATE LEG, SPIRITUALITY

Mission leaders' strongest leg, strategy, is directed and influenced by their intermediate leg, spirituality. They utilize their spirituality gifts to call the church to a deeper gospel, one that fulfills the mission of God in the world. Their spirituality makes sure that their strategy gift is in synch with the message and mission of Jesus.

Their intermediate leg, spirituality, is their secret weapon. Their spirituality leg gives depth to their strategy leg, by linking it to the power of the gospel message and attuning it to the movement of the Holy Spirit. Their intermediate leg is easier to develop than their weakest leg, because they are naturally stronger in that leg and have a better intuitive grasp of how to use it. Giving attention to developing consistent devotional habits and communicating the powerful gospel with passion are the most effective ways for them to become better Christian leaders. They should make sure they cultivate the three components of spirituality: saturation in Scripture, spiritual disciplines and sensitivity to the Holy Spirit.

DEVELOPING THEIR WEAKEST LEG, CHEMISTRY

God has given mission leaders natural abilities in strategy, but they feel less skilled in chemistry. This has the potential to sabotage otherwise good ministry or possibly get them fired. They need a respected mentor or coach who can give them wise counsel and offer accountability in their development of chemistry. It is important to consider the three spheres of chemistry—interpersonal chemistry, team chemistry and crowd chemistry—when developing a growth plan. Most mission leaders are strongest in interpersonal chemistry and weakest in crowd chemistry.

A common liability of mission leaders is their lack of people sensitivity. Their task orientation often keeps them from slowing down, listening to and empathizing with people. The primary reason mission leaders are low in chemistry is their action orientation. Their focus on vision distracts them from paying attention to group dynamics or caring for people's individual needs. Mission leaders can be insightful in counseling but may not want to commit much time to it.

By nature and habit, mission leaders spend 60 to 65 percent using their strategy leg, 25 to 30 percent using their spirituality leg, and only 10 to 15 percent using their chemistry leg. A more balanced approach would be a 50 to 30 to 20 ratio. This will improve with a better awareness of their time expenditure and a focus on establishing simple, consistent habits to develop their chemistry leg.

THE SHADOW SIDE OF MISSION LEADERS

Each of the six Christian leadership styles has two deep needs that are common to the style. These needs are deeply rooted within them, and the leader is usually unaware of them. Each of these hidden needs can have a positive aspect but also a more profound dark side. Mission leaders have a *deep need to overinnovate*. They love creativity, think imaginatively and generate new ideas that they want to implement immediately. However, they can change directions quickly and forget to consider the capacity of the leaders and members to adapt. They also have a *deep need to overwork*. Mission leaders usually have workaholic tendencies and can have a difficult time creating boundaries between their ministry life and their personal and family life.

THE TEN COMMANDMENTS FOR MISSION LEADERS

1. Focus on developing other leaders, especially younger leaders.

2. Learn from inspirational leaders how to rally people to support the mission.

3. Which of your colleagues or friends is strongest in chemistry? Ask that person to mentor and coach you in good chemistry habits.

4. Initiate friendships with relational leaders, who can help you develop better people-sensitivity instincts.

5. Schedule a half-day spiritual retreat once a month.

6. Find a trusted spiritual director or mentor to meet with regularly. Focus especially on your habits of prayer.

7. Be careful not to become a workaholic. Keep a proper balance between work, family, play and rest.

8. Use creative methods for Scripture study in order to keep your spirituality alive and growing. There are some great technology tools available to assist you.

9. Spend time each workday cultivating five to ten meaningful connections with your friends and colleagues through emails, texts or phone calls.

10. The complementary style for a mission leader is the imaginative leader. If you work at intentionally strengthening your spirituality, this will give you a second powerful leadership style for use in ministry.

LIFE SCRIPTURE FOR THE MISSION LEADER

I have worked much harder, been in prison more frequently, been flogged more severely, and been exposed to death again and again. Three times I was beaten with rods, once I was pelted with stones, three times I was shipwrecked, I spent a night and a day in the open sea, I have been constantly on the move. I have been in danger from rivers, in danger from bandits, in danger from my fellow Jews, in danger from Gentiles; in danger in the city, in danger in the country, in danger at sea; and in danger from false believers. I have labored and toiled and have often gone without sleep; I have known hunger and thirst and have often gone without food; I have been cold and naked. Besides everything else, I face daily the pressure of my concern for all the churches. (2 Cor 11:23, 25-28, describing Paul's life and experience in taking the mission of God throughout the Mediterranean world)

MISSION ASSIGNMENT—REFLECTING ON MISSION LEADERS

1. Describe a specific situation where a mission leader used his or her strategy gift to start a new mission or ministry for God. How did it make you feel? What was its lasting influence?

2. Pick one of the biblical characters listed above who was a mission leader. Describe how the person was most powerfully used by God.

3. Who do you know personally who might be a mission leader? Have that individual read this chapter, and ask him or her whether the description is accurate.

16

☀ The Imaginative Leader

Isn't it splendid to think of all the things there are to find out about?
It just makes me feel glad to be alive—it's such an interesting world.
It wouldn't be half so interesting if we know all about everything,
would it? There'd be no scope for imagination then, would there?

L. M. Montgomery

Imaginative leaders have an amazing gift of helping people engage
their culture by communicating the good news of Jesus in a way that is
fresh, creative and challenging to that culture.
Imaginative leaders are strongest in spirituality, intermediate in strategy
and weakest in chemistry. They are gifted by God to interact powerfully
with an innovative vision from God, and then lead people to step out
in faith to live out that new way of being the people of God. A verb to
describe their role is *create*. They use their spiritual creativity to synthesize new ideas and models, and then they use strategy to implement
their vision. Ephesians 4:11 lists five offices or gifts that a Christian
leader may have—apostle, prophet, evangelist, pastor and teacher.
Many inspirational leaders have the gift of a prophet.

Biblical examples of imaginative leaders are Daniel, Samuel and John
the Baptist. After having been taken as a captive to Babylon, Daniel
understood the culture of Babylon and became a prominent figure in
the Babylonian court. After the king, he was one of the three prominent
rulers in that country. Yet he challenged their culture by giving powerful
prophetic voice against the government that prevented the worship of

the true God. Imaginative leaders will benefit by studying the lives of these three biblical characters to better understand the character, behavior and style of imaginative leaders. Can you think of any other biblical characters who might be imaginative leaders?

Martin Luther King Jr., David Gibbons, G. K. Chesterton, Ravi Zacharias, Derwin Gray, C. S. Lewis, T. D. Jakes, Alexander Solzhenitsyn, Erwin McManus and Martin Luther are historic and contemporary examples of imaginative leaders. Reading their biographies and writings will give you new insights into how God can use you as an imaginative leader. What leaders do you know personally who have been imaginative leaders? How have you been influenced by them?

A term to describe the role of an imaginative lay leader is *ministry innovator*. These leaders are called to find new ways to engage the powerful gospel in their own culture and to help their church or ministry connect well with the new world in which they live.

Imaginative leaders will recognize many of the following characteristics in themselves: they are original, inventive, visionary, synthesizing, innovative, aesthetic, entrepreneurial, charismatic, cultural, creative, stimulating, avant-garde, inquisitive, leading edge, ingenious, artistic and stylish.

A friend of mine is pastor of a multiethnic church in urban Chicago. It is ten years old, with five hundred people in attendance, and the average attendee's age is thirty years old. It is very multiethnic, but the largest group is Asian-American. My friend is one of the best preachers I know. He has the ability to connect the gospel to the personal lives and struggles of his listeners, particularly those in the eighteen- to thirty-five-year-old age group. Each Sunday, he preaches a very thoughtful, challenging sermon that cuts right to the heart of the issues that his congregation faces each day, particularly the college students and young professionals. It is truly a life-transforming experience. He dresses well, fitting the avant-garde culture of the neighborhood of the church.

Another friend is one of the best preachers I have ever heard. As an associate pastor of the church we attended, she regularly was able to preach the Word of God to us. Her most memorable series was one that used a number of Beatles songs to frame a biblical and theological discussion of great importance. Since her husband was the worship leader at the church, the music and the sermon were integrated in such a way that you could not forget any of the songs and sermons. She loves God's Word and is an intelligent student of it.

I know another classic imaginative leader. He has a strong sense of what our culture needs so that Christianity can be powerful in that culture. He works hard at helping his congregation become an example of how the connection between the gospel and culture works itself out in both the community and the workplace, transforming both individuals and the culture.

God has created imaginative leaders with a unique way of leading. They have gifts specific to their own leadership style that are not natural strengths for other styles. By recognizing how they are gifted to lead, they will more readily understand their role in the kingdom of God. Understanding their style will help them know how they can be most effective as leaders in God's vineyard and more confident and aware of how God can use them to produce lasting fruit.

USING THEIR STRONGEST LEG, SPIRITUALITY

Imaginative leaders use their spirituality gift to envision a new way to live and serve as the people of God. They identify new trends in culture, then apply spirituality to discover creative ways to connect the people of that culture with the gospel. Imaginative leaders often have the ability to synthesize ideas from Scripture, theology, the arts, cultural trends and the values of the emerging generation to create a new way to live life as followers of Jesus.

Many imaginative leaders are gifted at communicating to large groups while they themselves are more introverted by nature. They need time alone or with a small group of creative friends to give birth to new ideas and structures. They know how to utilize creativity, innovation, surprise, the arts, music and compelling biblical truths to help Christians see their ministry context with new eyes.

Many imaginative leaders have a strong connection with cutting-edge culture. They love the arts, creative music and the latest style or fashion. Many imaginative leaders know how to attract a younger population without trying to be something they are not.

DEVELOPING THEIR INTERMEDIATE LEG, STRATEGY

Imaginative leaders' intermediate leg, strategy, is their secret weapon. Their strategy leg maximizes the power of their spirituality leg by turning their creative ideas into helpful ministry and organizational structures. The intermediate leg is always easier to develop than the weakest leg, as they are naturally stronger in that leg and have a better intuitive grasp of how to use it.

Imaginative leaders tend to have quick minds that can come up with new solutions to current problems. Their ability to envision the future and solve problems helps them use strategy as a tool for ministry progress.

Imaginative leaders are frustrated with a slow pace, resistance to change, routine activities, managing details, administration and frugality. Over time, their lack of interest in management can frustrate other leaders in their church or organization. Wise imaginative leaders rely on one or more trusted leaders who excel at management.

DEVELOPING THEIR WEAKEST LEG, CHEMISTRY

Their weakest leg, chemistry, has the potential to sabotage otherwise good ministry or possibly get them fired. It is the leaders' weakest leg that causes frustration with their performance and fruitfulness. To improve in this area, they need a respected mentor or coach who can give them wise counsel and provide accountability.

God gives imaginative leaders natural abilities in spirituality, but they are weakest in chemistry. While imaginative leaders can be amazing at crowd chemistry, many often experience challenges in interpersonal and team chemistry. The most common chemistry challenge of imaginative leaders is the need for increased relational wisdom. Often their heads are in the clouds, filled with great new ideas. Consequently, they miss critical relational clues sent by others.

Imaginative leaders can create frustration by quickly changing course without adequate notice. A common weakness of imaginative leaders is they may not understand the basic stability needs of most people, such as advanced notice, time to process change, proper financial planning and time investment in lay leaders.

Imaginative leaders are good at short-term personal relationships, but people may sense disengagement from the relationship as the imaginative leader "moves on" to the next great idea and new acquaintances. Another persistent challenge of imaginative leaders is that they do not intentionally ask questions and so may be unaware of the opinions or thoughts of others.

By nature and habit, imaginative leaders can spend 60 to 65 percent of their time using their spirituality leg, 25 to 30 percent using their strategy leg and only 10 to 15 percent using their chemistry leg. A more balanced approach would be a 50 to 30 to 20 ratio. This can improve through awareness of their time allotment and a focus on developing simple, consistent habits of exercising the chemistry leg.

THE SHADOW SIDE OF IMAGINATIVE LEADERS

Each of the six Christian leadership styles has two deep needs that are common to that style. These hidden needs are deeply rooted, and the leader is usually unaware of them. For imaginative leaders, the first is a *deep need to be right*. They believe they are right on most subjects and often subtly ignore others' opinions and thoughts. The other is a *deep need to overinnovate*. They love creativity, think imaginatively and come up with many new ideas, which they want to implement immediately. However, they often head in a new direction without considering the capacity of other leaders and members to switch directions as quickly.

The shadow side of imaginative leaders is spiritual pride, oversensitivity or excessive self-criticism. Spiritual pride occurs when they compare themselves to others and consider themselves more insightful than and superior to other Christians. Imaginative leaders are often overly sensitive to criticism and can be too critical of themselves. They set high personal standards and experience excessive guilt and self-condemnation when they fall short of the ideal. Imaginative leaders can also react negatively to correction or criticism from others.

THE TEN COMMANDMENTS FOR IMAGINATIVE LEADERS

1. Develop better self-awareness by asking trusted friends incisive questions about yourself.

2. Overinnovation can be a weakness for an imaginative leader. Who are you accountable to, so that your innovation does not become excessive?

3. Which of your ministry colleagues is strongest in interpersonal communication and chemistry? Meet with and learn from him or her.

4. Make sure your team activities include time for chemistry and fun.

5. Take a half-day spiritual retreat once a month, if possible with other Christian leaders.

6. Find a trusted spiritual director or mentor to meet with regularly.

7. Make sure you get regular, accurate feedback from your staff, lay leaders and members.

8. Who is an experienced Christian leader you know who is gifted with wisdom? Meet with that person and learn from him or her.

9. Make sure that you intentionally maintain strong relationships with your best friends. Regularly having fun with friends and praying with them will help you balance your life.

10. The complementary style of an imaginative leader is the mission leader. If you increase your knowledge and time investment in strategy, this will give you a second powerful leadership style to utilize in ministry.

LIFE SCRIPTURE FOR THE IMAGINATIVE LEADER

For this reason, ever since I heard about your faith in the Lord Jesus and your love for all God's people, I have not stopped giving thanks for you, remembering you in my prayers. I keep asking that the God of our Lord Jesus Christ, the glorious Father, may give you the Spirit of wisdom and revelation, so that you may know him better. I pray that the eyes of your heart may be enlightened in order that you may know the hope to which he has called you, the riches of his glorious inheritance in his holy people, and his incomparably great power for us who believe. That power is the same as the mighty strength he exerted when he raised Christ from the dead and seated him at his right hand in the heavenly realms, far above all rule and authority, power and dominion, and every name that is invoked, not only in the present age but also in the one to come. (Eph 1:15-21)

MISSION ASSIGNMENT—REFLECTING ON IMAGINATIVE LEADERS

1. Describe a specific situation in which an imaginative leader used his or her spirituality gift to challenge the worldview of our culture or started a new church or ministry that really connected with the young generation. How did it make you feel? What was its lasting influence in your life?

2. Pick one of the biblical characters referenced in this chapter who was an imaginative leader. Describe how the person was most powerfully used by God.

3. Who do you know personally who might be an imaginative leader? Have that individual read this chapter, and ask him or her whether the description is accurate.

All Christian leaders need mentoring and coaching, especially when they are younger leaders. Often people do not understand the difference between the two. A simple way to describe the difference using this leadership model's language is that mentoring focuses on spirituality and the seat of leadership wisdom, while coaching focuses on strategy and chemistry. The reason for this differentiation is that mentoring has much more to do with a person's inner life, while coaching has much more to do with his or her behavior and actions. Spirituality and wisdom are internal qualities, whereas chemistry and strategy are more external traits.

Mentoring focuses on the spirituality leg and the seat of leadership wisdom. Mentoring directs its attention on who a person will become. Mentoring follows the leadership principle of Paul, "Follow my example, as I follow the example of Christ" (1 Cor 11:1). When you mentor someone, you are asking him or her to emulate your life, with the stipulation that you are intent on following the example of Christ in your own life.

Mentoring focuses on character, personal transformation and wisdom. The goal of mentoring is to produce deeper and wiser leaders. Paul describes this when he writes, "My dear children, for whom I am again in the pains of childbirth until Christ is formed in you"(Gal 4:19). Mentoring focuses on Christ being formed in the person—his or her internal development as a person. Jesus is our role model for our development in spirituality and leadership wisdom.

John 15 is a great spirituality chapter in the Bible. The book of James is a great wisdom book in the New Testament. When you mentor people in spirituality and wisdom, these two teachings can give them a written picture of the end product of good mentoring.

Coaching focuses on strategy and chemistry. Coaching directs its attention on the "who and how" of ministry development. Coaching focuses on developing strategic plans to connect people to one another and to produce lasting physical ministry for God. There is a physicality to coaching. The goal of coaching is to produce leaders who are stronger both in human connections and in strategic plans and their implementation. Paul and Barnabas are two excellent role models for strategy and chemistry, respectively.

Romans 16 is a great chemistry chapter. Romans 15 is a great strategy chapter. When you coach people in chemistry and strategy, these two chapters can give them a written picture of the end product of your coaching.

When you coach and mentor, you will find that viewing a person's online leadership style report is extremely helpful. Even if you know the person well, you will find out much more about who they are, how God has gifted them and how they lead by reading their profile.

Here are a few thoughts about interpreting their scores. First, what is the meaning of a low score? When a person has a score under 50 in any of the legs or the seat, it means that to become a better leader, they need coaching and/or mentoring in that area. The first assumption you should make is that they have fewer intuitive instincts combined with lax habits in that area. They need to know from their mentor or coach what to do and who to emulate. The primary solution for leadership growth when a score is under 50 is the development of better habits and more accountability. Your role in their life will help them develop better habits as a leader. If you are mentoring, you primarily want to look at the scores of spirituality and leadership wisdom (the second is found in the green chart on page three of their report). If you are coaching, you primarily want to look at the scores of strategy and chemistry.

What is the meaning of high scores? Scores over 70 typically mean that a person has both gifts and good habits in that area.

What does it mean when a person gets high scores in all three legs of their profile? It means the person is either very good in each area, or is rather delusional about their own gifts and abilities. Understanding which one it is will be very helpful for you as a mentor or coach! An important rule of thumb is that the less experience or fruitfulness a leader has had in their life, the higher they often rate themselves. You

can usually decide which one it is by comparing their ministry experience and the details of their fruit produced in specific areas of ministry with their rating of themselves. If you decide that they are over-
estimating their strength in a particular area, it is important to be able
to process with them that a high score can mean that the person has
rather low standards for themselves and doesn't yet understand how
much more growth is possible for them in that area.

The Six Style website has a valuable inventory that assesses a
Christian leader using a 360-degree evaluation process, with this leadership model as the guide for evaluation and understanding. It is designed to be safe for the person assessed, while providing that person
and his or her supervisor with useful and productive feedback. You
can take advantage of this online "Mentoring and Coaching Tool" by
taking it yourself, or by using it to help you coach and mentor another
leader. Go to sixstyles.org/coachingtool.php. There is a nominal cost
for this inventory.

DEEPER INTO
THE SIX STYLES

Section Four gives depth and detail to the six styles of Christian leaders. Each of the six chapters looks at the six styles through a different perspective. This will help you understand your style better, as well as enrich your awareness of how other leaders with different styles function. It will explain so much that has hitherto been so murky for you! Each chapter will help you understand and appreciate a key word that defines who you are. You will see how other styles are wired by God to have contrasting gifts from yours. It will enrich your appreciation of God's creativity and the beautiful diversity within his creation.

17

The Six Styles and Spiritual Gifts

I believe God made me for a purpose,
but he also made me fast. And when
I run I feel His pleasure.

Eric Liddell

H ow do the six Christian leadership styles correlate with the discussion of spiritual gifts in the Bible? While the New Testament mentions up to twenty-three spiritual gifts, few churches find that spiritual gift inventories help people learn how to use their gifts in real-life situations. There is a simpler solution to applying giftedness in specific ministry functions.

The Leadership Stool model is closely tied to the five gifts mentioned in Ephesians 4:11-12: "So Christ himself gave the apostles, the prophets, the evangelists, the pastors and teachers, to equip his people for works of service, so that the body of Christ may be built up." This passage has always played an important part in the discussion of spiritual giftedness. Recently, author Alan Hirsch has helped refocus on this emphasis in the broader church and has reenergized the discussion through his books. Figure 17.1 shows how the six Christian leadership styles match up with the Ephesians 4:11 gifts.

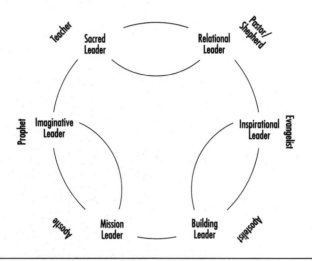

Figure 17.1. The six styles and Ephesians 4:11 gifts

✳ **Inspirational leaders** often have the gift of an evangelist. Their social intelligence helps them attach with people, in both personal and crowd contexts. Evangelism comes naturally to them because of their social ease, their intrinsic motivation to relate to people far from God and their intuitive ability to properly engage in a meaningful conversation. Churches led by inspirational leaders typically see much evidence of fruitful evangelism, in part because the inspirational leaders appear to be easily accessible to people who are not Christians.

💬 **Relational leaders** often have the gifts of shepherding or pastoring. Their interpersonal intelligence helps them connect to people in a warm and caring manner. They are attentive to the needs of people and good at pastoral care. They know how to love people! Relational pastors often pastor relational churches. These churches are especially common in town and country settings but can be found in many urban and suburban locations as well. These churches specialize in creating a warm atmosphere of fellowship and inclusion. (See chapter 21 for a discussion of the six styles of churches.)

The relational leader uses his or her interpersonal skills to communicate this warmth and provides a caring, listening ear for all.

✚ **Sacred leaders** often have the gift of teaching. Their greatest gift to the church is communicating to people the deep things of God. As teachers, they prepare well and deliver thoughtful and spiritually enriching presentations. They often use the spiritual gifts of wisdom and discernment to accompany their teaching, and use their intrapersonal intelligence to move conversations from the shallow to the thoughtful. As teachers, sacred leaders have spiritual insight into Scripture and its application to a person's heart and life. As they deliver this through their teaching, Christians grow deeper in knowledge and wisdom while learning how to walk with God.

💡 **Imaginative leaders** often have the gift of a prophet. They like to look to the future and call the people of God to become who God created them to be. They create a vision and a path for the future while also speaking prophetically against any and all obstacles to embracing God's best. They use their cultural intelligence to relate to the emerging culture while prophetically challenging the entrenched culture. This necessarily means that prophets often speak against and dismantle the dysfunctions and fossilized structures of the past. They call out hardness of heart, intransigent attitudes and culture-bound Christianity. This produces both committed followers and alienated detractors. Lukewarm does not work for them!

↑ **Mission leaders** often have the gift of an apostle. This gift creates the ability to lead the mission of God into the future through the development of ministries, ministers (both professional and lay) and mission endeavors. Apostles like to be out in the field, catalyzing vision and mobilizing people for what God is about to do. They are future-oriented, seeking to work with God to create the "new." They like variety and seldom stay in one location their whole life. If there are no new challenges to accomplish, they will die on the inside. The mission leader likes ideas but especially wants to leave behind the physical results of productive and visionary leadership. The fruit of an apostolic gift is new churches, new ministries and new leaders.

⬛ The apostle Paul only identified five gifts, while the Leadership Stool model produces six styles of Christian leadership. This difference in numbers is solved by recognizing that **building leaders**, situated between the mission leader and the inspirational leader styles, often have *a portion* of the gifts of both an apostle and an evangelist. The word to describe this hybrid is a contraction of both—an *apostelist*. Their primary love is growing the church or organization they serve, while simultaneously making it better and stronger. They are pragmatic visionaries. They typically stay in one location for an extended period of time and never tire of creating "more" and "better." Because building leaders have organizational intelligence, they focus on strategy and structure. Like the mission leader, they want to make physical progress, which for them often translates into more staff, more people and more buildings. Like the inspirational leader, they evidence a strong desire to see more people become Christians, but they use strategy more than chemistry to accomplish that goal.

You can use these Ephesians 4:11 gifts to identify which Christian leadership style a particular person possesses. Is the person gifted in evangelism? Then he or she is most likely an inspirational leader. Is he great at caring for people? Then he may be a relational leader. Does she love teaching about God? Then she could be a sacred leader. Is he innovative and prophetic? Then he's most likely an imaginative leader. Is she always thinking about multiplying the ministry? Then she might be a mission leader. Is the person focused on growing the church or organization? Then that individual is most likely a building leader. Identifying a person's gift can help you identify that individual's leadership style.

German New Testament scholar Johannes Reimer offers very insightful thoughts about how the Ephesians 4:11 vision can be implemented in a church. He gives this simple description to identify which specific task the Ephesians 4:11 gifts are correlated with in building up a church or Christian organization:

◆ The mission leader (apostle) sets the agenda.

◆ The imaginative leader (prophet) analyzes the target (the culture).

◆ The inspirational leader (evangelist) leads people to Christ.

◆ The relational leader (pastor) disciples the converts.

◆ The sacred leader (teacher) lays the scriptural foundation.

◆ The building leader (apostelist) grows the church.[1]

The mission leader (apostle) and the imaginative leader (prophet) have a voice and ministry to spread the larger vision of God at work in the world and how that vision relates to and challenges culture. These leaders often use their gifts beyond the normal confines of a local church. The mission leader (apostle) has a vision of God's future for a particular ministry area, a people group or a geographical area. The imaginative leader (prophet) helps the church learn how to connect with the emerging culture, while speaking a prophetic word against all worldviews and cultures that destroy God's good creation and diminish his perfect will.

The remaining four styles and gifts are given to the local church. These are the four that help a church do fruitful ministry "on the ground." The inspirational leader (evangelist) leads people to Christ. This always has to be the beginning point of local mission. Without evangelism, a church is dead in the water, both in the present and in its future. Then, relational leaders (pastors) disciple the converts. They use their chemistry gift to connect with each new Christian, while using their intermediate leg, spirituality, to lay down the basic foundations of the gospel, rooting each new Christian deeply in Christ.

Then, the sacred leader (teacher) lays down the scriptural foundations in the lives of Christians. This is disciple-making. These leaders help Christians become strong followers of Jesus, training their minds, their hearts, their wills and their actions to become complete disciples. They teach the message and mission of Jesus so that it becomes the message and mission of each disciple. Sacred leaders need to work in partnership with leaders who have the strategy gift to ensure that the church creates a comprehensive discipleship pathway, so that a high percentage of its attenders go both deeper in Christ and further in mission. Finally, the building leader (apostelist) grows the church. The healthy, missional church experiences a consistent forward momentum, asking that God may produce in them more disciples, among more populations, in a more caring and just world. Building leaders help make this a reality.

MISSION ASSIGNMENT—UNPACK YOUR EPHESIANS 4:11 GIFT

1. What is your Christian leadership style?

2. What is your complementary style?

3. How has the Ephesians 4:11 gift of your primary leadership style been manifested in your past ministry? Give specific examples.

4. How has the Ephesians 4:11 gift of your complementary leadership style been manifested in your past ministry? Give specific examples.

5. How can you envision God using these Ephesians 4:11 gifts even more in your future?

6. How will awareness of the six gifts help you be able to value and use all of them in strengthening your church or organization?

18

The Six Styles and Personality Tests

Leadership is not magnetic personality—that can just as well be a glib tongue. It is not "making friends and influencing people"—that is flattery. Leadership is lifting a person's vision to higher sights, the raising of a person's performance to a higher standard, the building of a personality beyond its normal limitations.

Peter Drucker

The Myers-Briggs Type Indicator (MBTI) is one of the most popular personality inventories now available and is familiar to many Christian leaders. StrengthsFinder was developed by the Gallup organization and is another popular tool for self-understanding. This chapter examines the correlations that exist between the six styles of Christian leadership, the sixteen Myers-Briggs types and the thirty-four talents in StrengthsFinder.

THE MYERS-BRIGGS TYPE INDICATOR

The Myers-Briggs Type Indicator has strong correlations with the six styles of Christian leadership. Table 18.1 shows how the different styles connect with the sixteen MBTI types.

This study is based on 943 leaders who took the Leadership Stool inventory and reported their Myers-Briggs type. Table 18.1 shows the sixteen Myers-Briggs types on the left, with the corresponding most common leadership style on the right.

Table 18.1. MBTI, with Its Most Frequent Leadership Style

MBTI	Most Frequent Leadership Style
ENFJ	Inspirational Leader
ENFP	Relational Leader
ENTJ	Building Leader
ENTP	Mission Leader
ESFJ	Relational Leader
ESFP	Inspirational Leader
ESTJ	Mission Leader
ESTP	Sacred Leader
INFJ	Imaginative Leader
INFP	Sacred Leader
INTJ	Building Leader
INTP	Mission Leader
ISFJ	Mission Leader
ISFP	(too small a sample)
ISTJ	Imaginative Leader
ISTP	(too small a sample)

Figure 18.1 shows the percentage of each of the sixteen Myers-Briggs types among Christian leaders, compared to the percentage of each type in the general population.

Figure 18.2 compares the relationship between the six leadership styles and the percentage that were intuitive or sensing in the MBTI. Intuitive feelers are by far the most likely people to enter ministry or serve in a lay leadership capacity. Intuitive thinkers come in a close second. Sensing people are very underrepresented in this sample of Christian leadership. This is all the more surprising, because 72 percent of the general population is sensing and only 28 percent intuitive. There has been much research that shows that the majority of Christian leaders and leaders in general are intuitive rather than sensing. This creates an interesting communications challenge in both churches and Christian organizations, as intuitive leaders try to communicate with intuitive ideas to sensing followers.

The following list describes which of the Myers-Briggs types are likely to be found in each of the six styles.

CHRISTIAN LEADERSHIP STYLES AND THEIR MOST FREQUENT MBTI TYPES

◆ Sacred leaders are likely to be INFPs, ESTPs and ESFJs.

◆ Relational leaders are likely to be ENFPs, ESTPs and ENFJs.

◆ Inspirational leaders are likely to be ENFJs, ESFJs and ESFPs.

◆ Building leaders are likely to be ENTJs, ENTPs and INTJs.

◆ Mission leaders are likely to be INFJs, ENTJs, ENTPs and INTPs.

◆ Imaginative leaders are likely to be INTJs, INFJs and ESTJs.

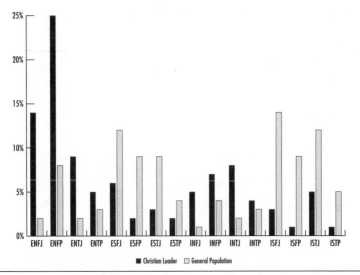

Figure 18.1. Percentage of Christian leaders vs. general population

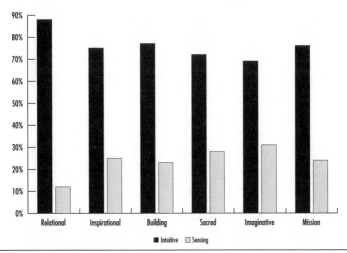

Figure 18.2. Intuitive and sensing in the six Christian leadership styles

The following list shows which Myers-Briggs types have the highest and lowest scores in spirituality, chemistry, strategy and leadership wisdom.

THE HIGHEST AND LOWEST LEADERSHIP LEG SCORES AND THE MBTI

◆ The highest spirituality scores were found in ENFJs, ENTJs and ESFPs.

◆ The highest chemistry scores were found in ENFJs, ENFPs and ENTJs.

◆ The highest strategy scores were found in ENTJs, INTJs and ENFJs.

◆ The highest leadership wisdom scores were found in ENTJs, ENFJs and ENTPs.

◆ The lowest spirituality scores were found in ISTJs, ISFJs and ENFPs.

◆ The lowest chemistry scores were found in ISTJs, ISFJs and INTPs.

◆ The lowest strategy scores were found in ENFPs, ESTPs and INFJs.

◆ The lowest leadership wisdom scores were found in ISFJs, ISTJs and INTJs.

STRENGTHSFINDER

StrengthsFinder is a popular inventory created by Gallup that evaluates your possible strengths based on thirty-four different talents and then reports your highest five talents. StrengthsFinder is very focused on both strategy and chemistry but has very little specific reference to spirituality, nor does it identify the two primary natural traits of spirituality people, artistry and ingenuity.

Tables 18.2-4 divide the talents into whether they are most similar to spirituality, chemistry or strategy. Each talent is listed (called a Strength Domain), then the need it fulfills on a team, the role of that person, and finally how it is manifested in a conflicted situation, as in the following sequence:

Table 18.2. Strength Domains Most Similar to Spirituality

Strength Domain	Needs on a Team	Needs as a Leader	Needs in Conflict
Belief	To hold to values	To provide a purpose	To keep things on track
Context	To know the background	To research history	To think about the past
Ideation	To see the big picture	To provide insight	To be creative

Table 18.3. Strength Domains Most Similar to Chemistry

Strength Domain	Needs on a Team	Needs as a Leader	Needs in Conflict
Adaptability	To have flexibility	To live in the moment	To go with the flow
Communication	To tell their story	To be great presenters	To be heard
Connectedness	To see relationships	To provide hope and faith	To supply rationale
Developer	To encourage others	To cultivate growth in others	To recognize improvements
Empathy	To understand others	To tune into others	To sense others' feelings
Harmony	To achieve consensus	To promote collaboration	To look for agreement
Includer	To invite others in	To accept others	To include others
Individualization	To appreciate uniqueness in people	To appreciate unique contributions	To recognize varying viewpoints
Relator	To be close to others	To deepen relationships	To remain connected
Woo	To win others over	To network with others	To be energized by challenge
Positivity	To engender enthusiasm	To get buy-in from others	To keep things upbeat

Table 18.4. Strength Domains Most Similar to Strategy

Strength Domain	Needs on a Team	Needs as a Leader	Needs in Conflict
Achiever	To challenge	To be productive	To make it productive
Activator	To learn by doing	To make things happen	To be impatient
Analytical	To think critically	To assess situations	To see all sides
Arranger	To design a plan	To configure for productivity	To be flexible
Command	To make decisions	To take control	To move conflict forward
Competition	To be the best	To want to be the best	To win
Consistency	To encourage fairness	To treat people equally	To set up clear rules
Deliberative	To assess risk	To anticipate obstacles	To help make decisions
Discipline	To organize	To create order	To add structure
Focus	To keep goal in mind	To prioritize and follow through	To stay on track
Futuristic	To have a vision	To inspire others	To focus on what could be
Input	To collect information	To desire to know more	To ask for the facts
Intellection	To think	To be introspective	To encourage discussions
Learner	To learn	To want to improve	To focus on the process
Maximizer	To achieve excellence	To focus on strengths	To seek to improve
Restorative	To solve problems	To assess challenges	To help resolve differences
Responsibility	To follow through	To do it right	To be honest and loyal
Self-assurance	To be right	To provide confidence	To influence outcome
Significance	To make a difference	To strive to stand out	To be recognized
Strategic	To find the best route	To forge the path forward	To quickly name the issues

In summary, the MBTI is very helpful as a personality test and has some application to leadership ability. However, it is focused on personality type rather than leadership style, so it only has secondary ability to describe how people of a certain type may lead. There are clear correlations between many of the Myers-Briggs personality types and the six styles of Christian leaders.

StrengthsFinder has more direct applicability to evaluating leadership ability, but the high number of strength domains make it difficult to use the model as a clear and simple tool for leadership development. Inability to incorporate some of the qualities of Christian spirituality into its worldview also limits its value for Christian leaders.

Much more on the relationship between the six styles of leadership and the Myers-Briggs inventory or the StrengthsFinder inventory can be found at sixstyles/personality.php.

MISSION ASSIGNMENT — UNPACK HOW YOUR STYLE CORRESPONDS WITH YOUR PERSONALITY

1. How does your leadership style fit with your Myers-Briggs type?

2. How does your leadership style fit with your StrengthsFinder profile?

3. How does the addition of spirituality create a richer understanding of how God has made you?

19

The Six Deep Needs
of Leaders

*Confront your inadequacies
and push your personal boundaries:
It's the surest way to grow, improve and
expand the scope of your influence.*

John Maxwell

Each of the six Christian leadership styles has two deep needs
that are common to that type. These needs are deeply rooted,
and the leader is often unaware of them. Each of these needs has a
positive benefit but also a more profound dark side. These deep needs
significantly affect the motivations and behaviors of leaders and have
an important effect on how they lead and minister, sometimes for good
and sometimes for ill.

The two deep needs that each leadership style possesses are shown
in figure 19.1.

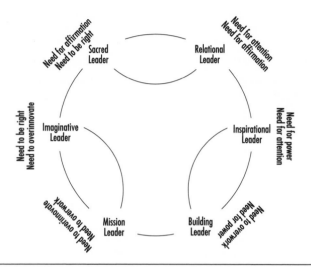

Figure 19.1. The six hidden needs of Christian leaders

✟ SACRED LEADERS

Sacred leaders have a *deep need for affirmation.* Most people do not recognize or fulfill this emotionally important need of a sacred leader. They need to receive specific words of encouragement from friends and colleagues. This is one of the most important gifts that people can give to a sacred leader. The difficulty sacred leaders have in receiving affirmation may be rooted in the fact that they are more aware than most how much they fall short of the glory of God. While this is valuable in maintaining humility, it creates resistance to the proper receiving of deserved praise.

Sacred leaders also need to reciprocate through giving encouragement to others. By nature, most are rather sparing in their compliments to others. Again, this may be because of their aversion to all expressions that promote prideful thoughts.

Sacred leaders should ask themselves this question: "What causes my deep need for affirmation?"

Sacred leaders also have a *deep need to be right.* They intuitively believe they are right on most subjects external to themselves and may ignore or diminish other opinions and thoughts. Many times they are right. Their intrapersonal intelligence helps them understand complex situations and read people's motivations in ways that others do not see. However, their tacit assumption that they are always right keeps them from hearing and seeing other people's perspectives and ideas.

Sacred leaders should ask themselves this question: "What causes my deep need to be right?"

🗩 RELATIONAL LEADERS

Relational leaders have a *deep need for attention*. They love to be around people, and they prosper in an environment that is filled with love and harmony. Solitary confinement would be the worst possible punishment for a relational leader. People are their "food and drink," and they perish without large doses of human interaction. They love interpersonal chemistry, relish being on a team and enjoy being a part of a crowd. Their need for attention also causes them to please people and to strongly dislike being ignored. All of these factors help to explain why they are so adept at human relationships.

Relational leaders should ask themselves this question: "What causes my deep need for attention?"

They also have a *deep need for affirmation*. They are more aware of this need than the sacred leader. Relational leaders need to receive specific words of encouragement from friends and people of influence. This is one of the most important gifts that a person can give a leader. They themselves are good at giving encouragement to others but need a lot of encouragement in return.

Relational leaders should ask themselves this question: "What causes my deep need for affirmation?"

💥 INSPIRATIONAL LEADERS

Inspirational leaders have a *deep need for power*. They love to have influence but also like control. Inspirational leaders can exercise inordinate power in a church or organization. They usually acquire power through their ability to joyfully persuade people to let them decide. They typically employ a group process to allow people to participate in planning but are quite skilled at getting their way by the end of the meeting. Developing the habits of asking questions and listening carefully are powerful antidotes to the need for power.

Inspirational leaders should ask themselves this question: "What causes my deep need for power?"

Inspirational leaders also have a *deep need for attention*. All leaders strongest in chemistry have this need. Inspirational leaders also have a need to please people, which is why they shine in front of a crowd. While this can have its benefits, it may be motivated by self-centeredness, or more often by insecurity. Leaders who are strongest in chemistry need to be aware of the potential seduction of the need for attention and guard against it.

Inspirational leaders should ask themselves this question: "What causes my deep need for attention?"

■ BUILDING LEADERS

Building leaders have a *deep need to overwork*. They often have difficulty drawing boundaries between their work life and their personal life because they want to accomplish as much as possible for God. They set high goals, make the plans needed for organizational growth, recruit people to do the work and spend most of their emotional energy fulfilling the task. Because they are so productive, their responsibilities continually expand, resulting in overwork. Without establishing and monitoring strong boundaries between their professional life and their personal life, they risk placing their work before their marriage and family.

Building leaders should ask themselves this question: "What causes my deep need to overwork?"

They also have a *deep need for power*. The positive side of power is having the ability to influence. The negative is the need for control. Building leaders need to be aware of how they use power. They should focus on the influence side rather than the exercising control side. Because they have such clear goals for the organization and high needs for accomplishment, they are tempted to control everything. The best strategy to regulate the need for power is to ask discerning questions of other leaders, giving them permission to speak words of challenge. In organizational decisions, building leaders should allow both the group and their own influence to have equal effect on the decision.

Building leaders should ask themselves this question: "What causes my deep need for power?"

➤ MISSION LEADERS

Mission leaders have a *deep need to overinnovate*. They love creativity, think imaginatively and come up with many new ideas that they want to implement immediately. Because of their unrestrained drive to create, mission leaders have difficulty discerning which of their ideas are realistic and helpful, and which demand too much of their people's energy and motivation. They can quickly embrace a new direction without considering whether it will work, what it will require, or the capacity of the leaders and members to switch directions that quickly.

Mission leaders should ask themselves this question: "What causes my deep need to overinnovate?"

They also have a *deep need to overwork*. Mission leaders usually have workaholic tendencies and have difficulty separating their ministry life from their personal and family life. They continually generate new ideas and expect to act on them immediately. Often they bite off much more than they can chew. As with the building leader, their job responsibilities continually grow. Mission leaders need to regularly learn to step back and determine which of their responsibilities and aspirations they should say no to. They need to weed the garden of their responsibilities regularly.

Mission leaders should ask themselves this question: "What causes my deep need to overwork?"

-💡- IMAGINATIVE LEADERS

Imaginative leaders have a *deep need to be right*. They believe they are right on most subjects and may ignore or diminish other opinions and thoughts. Because they believe their creative ideas are from God, it is hard for them to share ownership of their ideas with other people or to allow their ideas to be evaluated and improved. Their tacit assumption that they are always right prevents them from hearing and seeing other people's helpful perspectives.

Imaginative leaders should ask themselves this question: "What causes my deep need to be right?"

They also have a *deep need to overinnovate*. Imaginative leaders also love creativity, think imaginatively and generate new ideas that they want to implement immediately. They can quickly embrace a new direction without evaluating the wisdom of the change, the amount of work it will require, or the capacity of leaders and members to change directions quickly. Their lack of interest in management also can frustrate other leaders in their church or organization.

Imaginative leaders should ask themselves this question: "What causes my deep need to overinnovate?"

MISSION ASSIGNMENT — UNPACK YOUR DEEP NEEDS

1. Which of your deep needs is most prevalent?

   Is it accurate?

   Where does it come from?

   How often does it cause you difficulties?

   How can you become more aware of this deep need?

   What practical steps can you take to diminish the potential downside of this deep need?

2. List your other deep need.

   Is it accurate?

Where did it come from?

How often does it cause you difficulties?

How can you become more aware of this deep need?

What practical steps can you take to diminish the potential downside of this deep need?

20

The Six Intelligences
of Leaders

Intelligence is quickness in seeing things as they are.

George Santayana

A leader is one who sees more than others see,
who sees farther than others see,
and who sees before others do.

Leroy Eims

There are many types of intelligences that are listed by personality specialists. For example, on the Internet you can find out about linguistic intelligence, logical-mathematical intelligence, spatial intelligence, bodily-kinesthetic intelligence, musical intelligence and naturalistic intelligence.

I have discovered that each of the six styles of Christian leadership possess a particular type of intelligence. These intelligences are not an IQ type of intelligence but are more related to emotional intelligence. They give a person special insight into understanding what is happening within a particular environment or situation or person. Each intelligence helps the leader use his or her leadership style in a more powerful way.

SUMMARY

Sacred leaders have *intrapersonal intelligence*.
Relational leaders have *interpersonal intelligence*.
Inspirational leaders have *social intelligence*.
Building leaders have *organizational intelligence*.
Mission leaders have *strategic intelligence*.
Imaginative leaders have *cultural intelligence*.

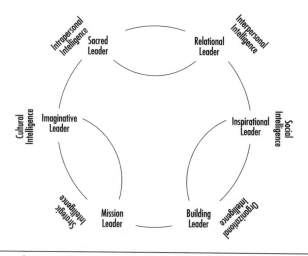

Figure 20.1. The six intelligences of Christian leaders

✚ SACRED LEADERS: INTRAPERSONAL INTELLIGENCE

Sacred leaders have gifts in intrapersonal intelligence, which is the ability to understand the thoughts, emotions and motivations within another person.

Their two-word description is *discerning wisdom*.

What? The sacred leader's intrapersonal intelligence can often seem supernatural. These leaders are able to see into the heart of another person. Other words to describe this intelligence are intuition, discernment and wisdom. It is a gift from God.

Where? Because intrapersonal intelligence can be misused, it is best applied in a somewhat private setting with an individual. It often occurs in a personal discussion, in a situation where advice and counseling is given or during a spiritual direction or mentoring session. It is most powerful when there is an atmosphere of trust. When meeting with an individual, a cup of coffee or tea can help set the mood.

When? Sacred leaders often keep many of their "God gifts" to themselves. They can be reserved or even hesitant to put themselves in a situation in which they would naturally use this intelligence. To use this gift, sacred leaders need to listen for God's direction and have the courage to place themselves with people and in situations where they can use their gifts.

How? Sacred leaders need to be careful about how they use their intrapersonal intelligence. Declarative statements can often be heard as judging, which creates resistance in the listener. Instead, sacred leaders should explore their perceptions by gently asking questions. Sacred leaders often follow this progression in their questioning: first, they allow the receiver to give voice to his thoughts; then they help him process his feelings and finally they help him reveal the motivations of his heart. Sacred leaders can use what they learn with individuals to help them become better communicators with groups and crowds. As they guide a group or crowd, sacred leaders can be good at helping people wrestle with their thoughts, feelings and motivations, which will help participants create a space in their hearts for God to work.

Why? Sacred leaders have an important message to deliver to an individual, a group or a crowd. Their gift is to help people connect with the deep things of God. Intrapersonal intelligence is the tool given to them by God to help guide people into their own deep places, so they can have an honest and often profound conversation about how God wants to dwell in them. It is important that sacred leaders use their intrapersonal intelligence to understand what the receiver needs and why the receiver may be resistant to go to a deeper place.

● RELATIONAL LEADERS: INTERPERSONAL INTELLIGENCE

Relational leaders have interpersonal intelligence, which is the ability to understand relationship dynamics between individuals.

Their two-word description is *people connection.*

What? A relational leader's interpersonal intelligence makes him or her gifted at connecting with people. These leaders use good eye contact and a warm smile, and they radiate a genuine joy in seeing each person. They are exceptionally encouraging, cheerful and optimistic. They project love. Most relational leaders like to give physical expressions of love, such as shaking hands, hugging and back-slapping. They make you feel like one of their best friends. Their interpersonal intelligence helps them know how to do this.

Where? Their interpersonal intelligence makes them good in one-on-one environments and most social settings. They know how to work a room, while at the same time making every individual feel their personal and genuine attention. Relational leaders are good in almost any physical location or situation, such as a coffee shop, office or church fellowship hall. They like to be wherever other people are.

When? Relational leaders have great capacity for human interaction. They seldom feel exhausted by people. They are the "Energizer Bunny" of human relationships—they can go on and on and on.

How? Relational leaders are always on the lookout for people that they can connect with. One of their great contributions is their personal connection of love. They know how to create the glue that connects them to people, whether it is in their neighborhood, their community, their workplace, their children's activities or their church or Christian organization. They also have outstanding gifts when connecting with people they have just met. Spend five minutes with a relational leader, and you will feel like she is one of the best friends you have ever had!

Why? Relational leaders need to receive back from others what they give to people. They need to receive reciprocal love in equal measure to what they give so that their batteries can be recharged.

✸ INSPIRATIONAL LEADERS: SOCIAL INTELLIGENCE

Inspirational leaders have social intelligence, which is the ability to understand the relationship dynamics of a group or a crowd.

Their two-word description is *group motivator*.

What? Inspirational leaders understand social hierarchy and will cater to a wide variety of people—the most needy, the most important, the newest, the most powerful, the hippest or the most fun. They are good at creating inclusion and know how to feed the group or crowd's energy.

Where? Inspirational leaders are most comfortable leading a crowd. They can be good leaders of teams, and, while they like people, they are often too busy to invest a lot of time with individuals. They like being with people who can make something happen.

When? Inspirational leaders give much thought to when important group events should happen. Their social intelligence helps them sequence the order and type of events so that there is a building sense of momentum.

How? Inspirational leaders understand momentum. They are always alert to whether or not the organization is moving forward. Their social intelligence first looks at the group's energy, dynamic and excitement, and makes sure the crowd and team chemistry are hot. They use the power of the crowd to do something great for God. Then they make sure there is something happening in the near future strategically that will inspire people. Social intelligence helps leaders create ownership in their people by letting them have a say in the direction of the organization.

Why? Inspirational leaders have a special ability to connect with people who are not yet Christians. Social, interpersonal and cultural intelligence can all help a leader connect with people who are seekers and skeptics. Inspirational leaders have a desire to make each connection count.

◼ BUILDING LEADERS: ORGANIZATIONAL INTELLIGENCE

Building leaders have organizational intelligence, which is the ability to understand how to structure an organization and then recruit the right people for the right positions.

Their two-word description is *efficient constructor*.

What? Building leaders want to create a structure in which everything works together with the least confusion or friction. They love systems. They do not like to be surprised. Organizational intelligence helps them achieve that.

Where? Building leaders like to work is settings with potential. It can be in a neighborhood or community that is flourishing, an organization that is poised for growth or a situation that has a lot of possible upsides.

When? Building leaders use their organizational intelligence in the present to plan for and change the future. They use organizational intelligence to accomplish physical progress in an expeditious manner. To do this, they are efficient, effective, streamlined and nonredundant, with their structures requiring clear lines of responsibility and accountability. Meetings should start on time and end on time. The agenda needs to be sent out in advance.

How? Building leaders like organizing everything. They organize their time, structures, details, lists, projects, people, clothes, and are even known to make sure their rolled socks in the drawer all point in the same direction! In order to make the organization work, they need people. They want to help these people know what to do and how to fit the structure well. They are very optimistic and cheery when recruiting, because they know people are critical to their organizational goals.

Why? Building leaders are built to grow organizations. Many of the Bible's best stories are about growth and organization. Jethro helping Moses understand delegation, Gideon recruiting a highly focused rapid deployment team, Ezekiel's vision of the restoration of Israel, the plan to distribute the bread in the feeding of the five thousand and the care of widows by the early church all illustrate organizational intelligence at work. Building leaders serve in an expansionist religion, always believing in "more and better" as a noble goal.

↑ MISSION LEADERS: STRATEGIC INTELLIGENCE

Mission leaders have strategic intelligence, which is the ability to understand how to envision the future and develop new structures and connections so that the future is fruitful.

Their two-word description is *focused multiplier*.

What? Strategic intelligence helps the mission leader see into the future and determine what needs to be created so that the future will be fruitful.

Where? Strategic intelligence focuses on new structures and systems that will increase fruitfulness for God. Mission leaders in particular see new opportunities, new people groups and new ministries that can reach people that are currently untouched by the message and mission of Jesus.

When? Mission leaders believe the time is now: "Now is the day of salvation" (2 Cor 6:2). Their strong strategic intelligence makes them impatient with waiting, because they know what could potentially happen in the future.

How? Mission leaders like to multiply. Their strategic intelligence helps them see the potential of going to a new people group in a foreign culture. They understand why starting a new church is so important for the health, vitality and future leadership of the larger church. They may see a need to start a new Christian relief agency or focus on recruiting and training young leaders. In all of these new ventures, their strategic intelligence is at work.

Why? Mission leaders are passionate about evangelism and spiritual depth. Their strategic intelligence can see trends, helping them know what will happen in the future if nothing changes. They want to upset the applecart and get beyond the old structure so they can innovate using a new structure.

IMAGINATIVE LEADERS: CULTURAL INTELLIGENCE

Imaginative leaders have cultural intelligence. This is the ability to understand the changing culture and know how to communicate Christianity so that it can both connect with and challenge that culture.

Their two-word description is *creative visionary*.

What? Most imaginative leaders possess cultural intelligence, which helps leaders understand the power and influence of their culture. Culture affects a person's worldview, philosophical assumptions and views of truth, goodness and beauty. It typically does this without the person's awareness that culture is shaping their foundational values. Therefore, the effect of culture is opaque to most people. Imaginative leaders know how to shape the culture so they can change the future.

Where? Imaginative leaders express their cultural intelligence through where and how they live. What they talk about, how they think, what music they listen to, the avocation they pursue, the clothes they wear and where they live are all expressions of their cultural intelligence. They want to be physically present in the conversations that drive intellectual and societal change.

When? Imaginative leaders know that this is the moment; without change, the present opportunity will disappear.

How? Cultural intelligence is expressed through fashion, music, artistry, ingenuity and the creative instinct. Imaginative leaders also have the ability to be prophetic toward their culture. They have discerning minds, ears, eyes and hearts to speak and act against anything that destroys God's good creation. Imaginative leaders can see when a church or Christian organization is out of step or irrelevant to contemporary culture, and they can help it to stay true to the gospel while making the changes needed to improve its connection with the culture.

Why? Imaginative leaders usually have the ability to be on the front end of cultural shifts by understanding and embracing the cultural changes that are particularly formative in the emerging generation. Cultural intelligence is a key factor in the attraction and retention of the younger generation.

MISSION ASSIGNMENT—UNPACK YOUR INTELLIGENCE

1. What is your type of intelligence? Do you like it?

2. How have you used it in the past? What specific areas does it make you very good in?

3. What can you learn by watching other leaders who have your style? How do they use their intelligence to advance the kingdom of God?

4. Knowing what you know now, how might you be able to use your intelligence to be even more fruitful for God's service?

21

The Six Styles of Churches and Christian Organizations

Only 20 percent of employees
working in large organizations surveyed
feel their strengths are in play every day.
Thus, eight out of ten employees surveyed
feel somewhat miscast in their role.

Stephen Covey

Just as there are six styles of Christian leaders, there are also six styles of Christian churches and organizations. Many of the mismatches that occur between leaders and their churches or organizations happen because leaders are not aware of their Christian leadership style and churches or organizations are not aware of their style. When the leader and the church or organization know each other's style and understand what it means to collaborate well, they have a much better chance of succeeding as a team.

The following are the six styles of churches and organizations. As you read them, it will be helpful if you are able to identify a church or Christian organization you know that fits each profile.

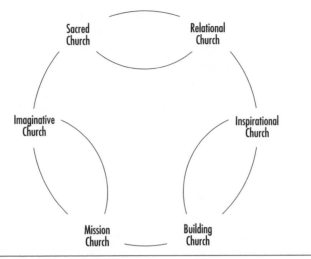

Figure 21.1. The six styles of churches

✚ THE SACRED CHURCH

The sacred church is gifted by God to connect spiritually with people and encourage them to grow deeper in God while paying attention to the voice of the Holy Spirit. Sacred churches are spiritually sensitive and want to focus their primary energy on loving God. They minister through their ability to genuinely connect with people by communicating the deep things of God. A primary focus of many sacred churches is teaching. They strive to create a strong scriptural and devotional foundation in the life of each member.

Sacred churches are described by others as being devout, Spirit minded, God loving, God fearing, reverent, virtuous, pure of heart, Christlike, peace loving, deep, reflective, contemplative, insightful, earnest and prayerful. They are confident that their message is from God. Some sacred churches are liturgical, and those that are more free in style maintain practices and rituals that are highly valued and seldom changed.

Sacred churches may face challenges with spiritual pride. This occurs when they perceive themselves to be more devout than other churches. They can also be judgmental toward churches that have a style different from their own. Sacred churches need to be careful that their rituals and spiritual practices do not become more important than the person of Jesus and his message and mission to the world.

Some sacred churches are so inwardly focused they may not be aware of the needs of the community around them. They are often not as open to outsiders, new ideas and change. Sacred churches have the highest percentage of introverts of any of the six church styles. They see fewer conversions to Christ than other types of churches, though they may desire for it to occur more frequently. They can also be so focused on their own depth and doctrine that they often don't perceive how others experience them.

Sacred churches often have a strong sense that their theology, practices and style are correct for every church. They believe that they hold the right biblical worldview and rituals, and they may ignore or diminish other expressions of belief and worship. A common challenge of sacred churches is their lack of practical usefulness. They often struggle to translate their deep spirituality into physical ministry in the community around them.

Sacred churches usually have an orientation toward the past. Memory and history are very important values to them.

REFLECTION QUESTIONS

1. Identify a sacred church you are familiar with. Would this be a church that would be life giving to you?

2. What would you perceive to be its strengths?

3. What would be its liabilities?

●THE RELATIONAL CHURCH

The relational church is gifted by God to help people connect emotionally with each other and to inspire them to follow Jesus and love each other. A word often associated with relational churches is *loving*. They facilitate caring relationships between people. Relational churches excel at providing a warm and safe environment where love and connection happens naturally. The majority of relational churches seldom grow beyond two hundred in attendance, so they truly are churches where everyone can know and be known by all. Relational churches are described by others as heartening, assuring, cheering, urging, exhorting, hopeful, sustaining, supporting and advocating. Relational churches are very good at encouraging people. They are gifted in connecting individuals with each other.

Relational churches utilize chemistry to create unity, joy and love in the group. Their leaders pay close attention to the reactions of individuals and know how to keep their members engaged through emotional investment. People in a relational church like to play, eat, talk, love, laugh out loud, care deeply, relate closely and display unity. An important role of relational churches is to live out the fruits of the Spirit in their relationships and ministry.

Relational churches emphasize people-helping ministries such as counseling, visitation and pastoral care. Relational churches have interpersonal intelligence and are sensitive to the relationship dynamics between individuals.

A common challenge of relational churches is their lack of clear focus. Their members love to connect with people but often do not know what the next step should be in their ministry development. Relational churches need to be challenged in both their spirituality and their strategy. They should ask themselves these two questions: "Are we being challenged to grow deeper in our knowledge of Scripture and our relationship with God? Are we so content with our own little group that we are not impacting the community around us?"

The relational church has an orientation toward the present, with a secondary focus toward the past.

REFLECTION QUESTIONS

1. Identify a relational church you are familiar with. Would this be a church that would be life giving to you?

2. What would you perceive to be its strengths?

3. What would be its liabilities?

✸ THE INSPIRATIONAL CHURCH

The inspirational church is gifted by God to motivate people to follow Jesus by engaging in the mission of God. They are known for their ability to influence people. Inspirational churches excel at getting people to rally around a vision. Inspirational churches know how to create an environment in which evangelism can occur.

The leaders in an inspirational church know how to mobilize people so that real ministry is accomplished in the world. Inspirational churches are described by others as inviting, invigorating, motivating, inspiring, activating and alive. Leaders in these churches use their chemistry gifts to create ownership and momentum in the church. They keep people mentally and emotionally engaged.

Inspirational churches often have the ability to grow rapidly. Their challenge is to create spiritual and structural depth that is commensurate with that growth. If the church gets bigger without its base becoming wider and deeper, the church will eventually lose its balance and stability. Inspirational churches are gifted at attracting people who are not yet Christians, and their people are trained to know how to engage them in conversations about God in a winsome way, which encourages further relationship and dialogue. Inspirational churches have many members who are gifted in social intelligence, which is the ability to create positive and engaging relational dynamics in the church or organization.

An inspirational church that sees many people become Christians plays an important role in the whole church today, as fruitful evangelism is becoming progressively more challenging as the culture changes. Inspirational churches should reflect on how and when this gift is used and how to maximize it. They need to create strong and reliable systems for the assimilation of and follow-up with new Christians so that they will become rooted in their faith.

For inspirational churches, an important component of their ministry fruitfulness is their promotional ability. However, other Christians and churches may view this type of church as shallow and self-promotional unless the church displays a commensurate depth of thought, wisdom and humility.

Leaders of inspirational churches use strategy to create ministry programs and momentum in their church and their community. They envision and build ministries that advance God's kingdom. They are highly motivated to create events and programs for people to grow as followers of Jesus, unstopped by human barriers. Inspirational churches are especially gifted in the strategic areas of thematic focus, sequential progression, event planning and team activities.

The primary weakness of inspirational churches is that their leaders and members are so busy connecting with outsiders and growing the church that they may neglect spending the time necessary for pursuing greater scriptural depth and intimacy with God. They should ask themselves, "Are we neglecting our relationship with God or are we growing in our intimacy with God?" Inspirational churches can also have a "star" mentality, especially when they honor the most successful and talented in their midst. They should ask themselves, "Do we really value all of our members and the gifts that each person brings to the whole?"

Inspirational churches have an orientation toward the present, with a secondary focus on the future.

REFLECTION QUESTIONS

1. Identify an inspirational church you are familiar with. Would this be a church that would be life giving to you?
2. What would you perceive to be its strengths?
3. What would be its liabilities?

THE BUILDING CHURCH

Building churches is gifted by God to strategize for growth and enlist people to enlarge the mission of God. They know how to grow in size, structure and facilities. They know how to create the right conditions and systems that produce numeric growth and an advancing ministry, so that more people come, join and serve. Many leaders in building churches or organizations have a growth gift. They have a green thumb for knowing how to create growth in the kingdom of God. They are focused on "more and better" and understand how to use vision, goals, structures, organization, hard work, energy and focus to bring about growth and development.

In the building church, a phrase that describes the role of many of its members is the *task accomplisher*. They are called by God to expand his kingdom through organizing and implementing specific tasks that produce more converts, better disciples and increased mission impact.

Building churches are described by others as focused, confident, direct, purposeful, convincing, inspiring, recruiting, visionary, planning, sequential, results oriented, persuasive, goal oriented, driven, expansionist and energetic.

Building churches usually exhibit a high degree of confidence in God's ability to work through them. Their leaders use mind power to plan for growth. They like to have the solution decided as quickly as possible. They move ahead in planning the timetable, people, structure and finances necessary to reach their goal. Building churches are excellent at envisioning the future and planning the sequential steps to get there. They have strong skills in both building and managing, which can sometimes give the perception that they function as a corporation.

Building churches always need to be moving forward, and they expect to continually grow and develop. Once the church or organization plateaus and begins to decline, they enter crisis mode until they get the momentum back.

Building churches are often so busy accomplishing that many of their members do not take the time to go deeper in Scripture and to grow in intimacy with God. It is important to consider the three core foundations of spirituality when developing a spiritual growth plan for these churches—saturation in Scripture, spiritual disciplines and sensitivity to the Holy Spirit. They should ask themselves, "Do we show compassion for our own people and for our community? Do we take time for quiet and reflection?"

Building churches have a primary orientation toward the future and a secondary orientation toward the present.

REFLECTION QUESTIONS

1. Identify a building church you are familiar with. Would this be a church that would be life giving to you?

2. What would you perceive to be its strengths?

3. What would be its liabilities?

⤴THE MISSION CHURCH

Mission churches are gifted by God to envision what needs to happen in the immediate future. They call people to follow a deeper gospel and then bring about the development of new expressions of the mission of God. They call people to live out an active gospel, while multiplying disciples, programs and ventures. Their best fruitfulness comes through reproducing new leaders, new ministries and new churches. Mission churches are the fruit producers in God's vineyard. Their leaders are quick to see possibilities for increased mission engagement, and they know how to use their activist ability to produce lasting fruit.

Mission churches are described by others as Spirit led, fruitful, productive, efficient, visionary, faith filled, disciple making, missionary, purposeful, catalyzing, envisioning, incisive, confident and assured.

Mission churches are motivated to turn ministry ideas into physical plans and action. The congregation can become impatient with too much group processing. They have a bias toward initiation and activity. Mission churches enjoy helping other churches become more effective in fulfilling the mission of God. They are gifted at removing obstacles as well as creating action plans that produce forward momentum. They like to focus on the critical issues, and when they have clarity they want to act quickly.

Mission churches like to ask the *what*, *when* and *how* questions: What should we be doing? When can we start? and How will we best accomplish the goal? They focus on building God's kingdom. Many mission churches have an intentional focus of their mission. They want to fulfill Jesus' prayer, "Your will be done, on earth as it is in heaven" (Mt 6:10).

Mission churches like to plan and then activate the plan. They want to create a strategy, whether it is for evangelism, feeding the hungry, training disciples, ending social problems, starting new ministries or planting new churches. Mission churches like to start ministries that do not now exist. They like to create new programs, new structures and new initiatives. Productivity and efficiency are two important values for mission churches. They like to use their time well and want to produce tangible results.

Mission churches have strategic intelligence, which is the ability to understand how to envision the future and develop new structures and connections so the future will be fruitful. Mission churches often start new churches in new geographical areas, cultures or people groups, or launch new ministries that meet an unmet need. Mission churches use their spirituality gifts to call the church and Christians to a deeper gospel, one that fulfills the whole mission of God in this world. Their spirituality makes sure that their strategy is correlated with the message and mission of Jesus.

A common challenge of mission churches is their lack of people sensitivity. Their strong task orientation and love for creating new structures often prevents them from empathizing with the people who need care. They should ask themselves, "Are we creating a sense of community in our church? Are we showing compassion to both our own people and our community and world?"

Most mission churches have an orientation toward the future.

REFLECTION QUESTIONS

1. Identify a mission church you are familiar with. Would this be a church that would be life giving to you?

2. What would you perceive to be its strengths?

3. What would be its liabilities?

☀ THE IMAGINATIVE CHURCH

The imaginative church is gifted by God to interact powerfully with a vision from God and then motivate people to step out in faith and live out that new way of being the people of God in their culture. Another term to describe imaginative churches is *creative*. They use their spiritual creativity to synthesize new ideas and models, and then use strategy to implement these imaginative ideas.

Many imaginative churches are prophetic, calling both Christians and the world to account. They are ministry innovators. They find new ways to engage the powerful gospel in their own culture so that they will connect well with the world in which they live.

Imaginative churches are described by others as original, inventive, visionary, innovative, aesthetic, entrepreneurial, cultural, creative, stimulating, avant-garde, inquisitive, leading edge, ingenious, artistic and stylish.

Imaginative churches use their spirituality gift to envision a new way to live and serve as the people of God. They identify new trends in culture and then apply spirituality to discover creative ways the gospel can connect with people who value those qualities. Imaginative churches often have the ability to synthesize ideas from Scripture, theology, the arts, cultural trends and the values of a new generation to create a new way to live life as followers of Jesus. They love the arts and creative music. Imaginative churches usually know how to attract a younger population, without trying to be something they are not.

Imaginative churches tend to be filled with leaders who have quick minds and can come up with new solutions to nagging problems. Their ability to envision the future and solve problems helps them use strategy as a tool for ministry progress. Imaginative churches usually don't like a slow pace, resistance to change, routine activities, managing details, administration and penny-pinching. However, over time, the lack of interest in the management side of strategy can undermine their good ministry.

Important questions for imaginative churches to ask are: "Do we lack stability because things change so rapidly? Does the staff feel cared for? Has our church developed a strong sense of intertwined community, especially through the use of routine and ritual?"

A common challenge of imaginative churches is their lack of relational wisdom. Their collective heads can be in the clouds, filled with great ideas, and they often miss critical relational clues sent by those in their midst.

Imaginative churches have an orientation toward the future, with a secondary focus on the present.

REFLECTION QUESTIONS

1. Identify an imaginative church you are familiar with. Would this be a church that would be life giving to you?

2. What would you perceive to be its strengths?

3. What would be its liabilities?

MISSION ASSIGNMENT — WHEN LEADER AND ORGANIZATION CLASH

Many of the conflicts between a leader and his or her church or organization are clashes between the leader's style and the church's style. The leader is called, not realizing the church's style may be very different from his or her own. The church does not realize that it has hired a leader with a completely different style from what it is used to.

Have you ever seen that situation?

How did it get resolved?

Did any collateral damage occur because of the clash?

How much better it would be if the church and the minister knew each other's style, personality, spiritual gifts, intelligence, deep needs and time perspective!

Balanced Leaders
Versus Focused Leaders

I want to compare faith to running in a race. It's hard. It requires
concentration of will, energy of soul. . . . And where does the power
come from, to see the race to its end? From within. Jesus said, "Behold,
the Kingdom of God is within you. If with all your hearts, you truly
seek me, you shall ever surely find me." If you commit yourself to the
love of Christ, then that is how you run a straight race.

Eric Liddell

An important theme throughout this book is the encouragement to achieve balance in the three legs of your leadership. This leadership model operates under the assumption that a three-legged stool is always most useful when it is balanced. And while I generally agree with that, this chapter will help you understand why only a small percentage Christian leaders have the ability to be truly balanced. The remainder of us need to keep developing our intermediate leg and shore up our weakest leg, but we will most likely always be focused leaders.

To help us understand this, we need to identify the two broad categories within Christian leadership styles: *balanced leaders* and *focused leaders*.

BALANCED LEADERS

Balanced leaders have the ability to lead more complex organizations, because they use their balanced strength in spirituality, chemistry and strategy to discern how to lead well in a wide variety of situations. Here is the criterion for knowing if you are a balanced leader: when all of your scores in the first chart are above the sixtieth percentile, and the percentage difference between your strongest and your weakest leg is 20 percent or less, you qualify as a balanced leader. Using this definition, only 6 percent of Christian leaders are balanced leaders.

Balanced leaders, by definition, have to be quite strong in all three legs—above the sixtieth percentile in spirituality, chemistry and strategy. Balanced leaders also need to have a certain evenness between the three scores—the difference between their strongest and their weakest leg has to be 20 percent or less. These are high standards, and very few leaders qualify as a balanced leader.

FOCUSED LEADERS

Focused leaders use their Christian leadership style in almost all situations. Learning to develop strength in your particular leadership style can help you become very strong at using your best gifts. Focused leaders are very effective in the specific niche of their style. Focused leaders are wise to identify and recruit a team of people who have complementary styles to balance them.

Focused leaders represent a much larger percentage of Christian leaders. When your highest score in the first chart is over the seventy-fifth percentile and your lowest score is under the fiftieth percentile, you are a *focused leader*. These criteria require that you are very strong in your strongest leg but definitely not as strong in your weakest leg.

BIBLICAL EXAMPLES

To help us understand this difference more fully, we will look at the lives and ministries of David, Jesus and Paul. In the Old Testament, I believe the most balanced leader was King David. The book of Psalms is a record of the spirituality of David. He wrote beautiful, heartfelt psalms to God that have resonated with believers down through the ages. They give voice to the spiritual experiences of all true seekers of God. He also showed his strength in strategy as a gifted leader for

Israel. And he possessed strong chemistry, which was demonstrated in the way his subjects adored him: "Isn't this David, the king of the land? Isn't he the one they sing about in their dances?" (1 Sam 21:11).

Jesus, of course, was the quintessential balanced leader. When I read through the pages of the Gospels, I see him functioning as each type of leader:

◆ a sacred leader (the Sermon on the Mount)

◆ a relational leader (with the woman at the well)

◆ an inspirational leader (Mt 11:28: "Come to me, all you who are weary and burdened, and I will give you rest")

◆ a building leader (Mt 16:18: "On this rock I will build my church")

◆ a mission leader (Mt 28:19: "Therefore go and make disciples")

◆ an imaginative leader (Jesus fulfilling the role of a prophet)

I believe Jesus possessed intrapersonal, interpersonal, social, organizational, strategic and cultural intelligence. I also believe Jesus manifested the gifts of apostle, prophet, evangelist, pastor and teacher in his dealings with people.

In chapter 15, I identified the apostle Paul as a mission leader. He would also be categorized as a focused leader. While he was greatly gifted in strategy and spirituality, his chemistry left something to be desired—although he was quite good at interpersonal chemistry. (If you need proof of this, just read Romans 16, where he describes in great detail his personal connections with dozens of Christians in Rome.) Yet it is apparent in the book of Acts and his letters that Paul could be a polarizing figure, and sometimes his lack of chemistry abilities created unnecessary challenges. Though he was strong in spirituality, I believe his natural instinct was even stronger in strategy. Yet, as a focused leader, Paul had the most influence of anyone in Christianity except Jesus.

CULTURAL EXAMPLES

In this book I have tried to highlight certain exceptional Christian leaders that I consider balanced leaders. In the research for this book,

I became even more impressed with the balance and wisdom of Dr. Martin Luther King Jr. Donald Phillips's book *Martin Luther King Jr. on Leadership*[1] is an amazing biography that makes it very apparent that Dr. King developed the skills to be equally strong in spirituality, chemistry, strategy and leadership wisdom. Although his natural Christian leadership style was the imaginative leader, the calling and requirements of the task at hand necessitated him becoming a balanced leader in order to rise to the demands of the moment.

I have been equally impressed with the balanced leadership of Henrietta Mears. The following quote shows how strong she was in strategy, spirituality and chemistry:

> The first thing I did in Hollywood [Presbyterian] was to write out what I wanted for my Sunday School. I set down my objectives for the first five years. They included improvements in organization, teaching staff, curriculums, and spirit. I wanted a closely graded program, a teaching material that would present Christ and His claims in every lesson, a trained teaching staff, a new education building, choirs, clubs, a camp program, a missionary vision, youth trained for the hour.[2]

Like Paul, Henrietta Mears was a mission leader, but I would categorize her as a balanced leader. She was strongest in strategy, leading the entire evangelical church in Southern California to develop structures and facilities that would multiply her ministry influence decades after her death. She knew how to create systems and training that allow the spiritual impact of the Bible to be built into the fiber of each student. She was also an incredible teacher who made Christ come alive for her students, which shows her strength in spirituality. And she understood and used her chemistry to great benefit throughout her life, as shown when she references how important it was to improve the "spirit" in the Christian education department of her church. Although she was a mission leader, she was that rare individual who could at the same time function as a balanced leader, using all three legs with great effectiveness. This allowed her overall influence to be much broader than if she confined herself to being only a focused mission leader.

In my own life, I have discovered that while I would love to be a balanced leader, in truth, I am much more of a focused leader. Like Paul and Henrietta, I am a mission leader. I score 85 in strategy, 69 in spirituality and 45 in chemistry. I recently held a position that required me to be more of a balanced leader. While I did my best, I am now back in a role that allows me to use my mission leader gift to its fullest. I can't tell you how much happier I am!

I began this chapter with a quote from Eric Liddell, gold medal winner of the 400-meter race in the 1924 Olympics. His story is portrayed in the 1981 Oscar-winning film *Chariots of Fire*. Liddell's specialty was the 100-yard dash. In 1923 he set a British record in that race at 9.7 seconds, which wasn't broken for twenty-three years. The crisis of the movie occurs at the Paris Olympics, when Liddell learns that the qualifying heat for the 100-meter race is scheduled for Sunday. Under heavy pressure to run on Sunday from the Olympic Committee and the Prince of Wales, he withdraws from the race and follows his convictions, refusing to break the sabbath.

Instead, he qualifies for and runs in the 400-meter finals, which was not his strongest event. A Highland pipe band plays as the race begins. At the starting block, an American Olympic Team masseur slips a note into his hand that says, "Those who honor me I will honor," a quote from 1 Samuel 2:30.

> The 400 metres had been considered a middle-distance event in which runners raced round the first bend and coasted through the back leg. Inspired by the Biblical message, and deprived of a view of the other runners because he drew the outside lane, Liddell raced the whole of the first 200 metres to be well clear of the favoured Americans. With little option but to then treat the race as a complete sprint, he continued to race round the final bend.[3] . . .
>
> Then the incredible happened. At the moment when any other runner would have started to flag, however determined, Eric Liddell somehow summoned up hidden reserves of strength and

stamina. Head back, chin forward, mouth open, knees jumping, arms waving, he put on a spurt and started to increase his lead over Fitch. At the tape, he was all of five meters ahead, and had won the Olympic title in a world record time of 47.6 seconds.[4]

Eric Liddell ran as a focused runner when he ran the 100-yard dash. Because of the demands of an exhausting 400-meter race, he needed to learn to run in a different way, as a balanced runner. His story reminds us that whether we lead as focused or balanced leaders, the task of Christian leadership requires something more than we can deliver through our own human strength.

MISSION ASSIGNMENT—ARE YOU BALANCED OR FOCUSED?

Are you a balanced leader or a focused leader?

When you reflect back on your ministry, how does this explain the details of where you were most fruitful?

If you are a focused leader, what does this say about the importance of recruiting and utilizing a balanced team?

SECTION FOUR ONLINE ACTIVITY: *SELECTING LEADERS*

"You live and die by who you hire." This is one of the most basic principles of leading a fruitful Christian organization. Make a great personnel choice, and life is good. When you hire a person who is self-motivated, has integrity and depth of character, is gifted to excel in the particular position, knows how to work well with people, is a hard worker and is self-aware and teachable—life is good! Have you ever made the wrong personnel choice? If so, you know about the pain, the frustration, the lack of progress, the hurt feelings and the loss of momentum.

Selecting the right leaders for volunteer positions within your church or Christian organization is equally as important. Do they have the gifts and experience for the particular role? Are they loyal and hard working? Will they work well with the team? What is their Six Style profile? Learning the answers to these and other questions will help you know whom to nominate for various positions and what is the right ministry role for each person.

The "Personnel Selection Tool" allows potential job candidates and volunteers to take a customized Six Style Inventory, as well as answer a series of questions, both of which will be forwarded directly to your church or organization. You will be able to gain new insight about the leadership styles and capabilities of the candidates for each position in your church or organization. Please go to sixstyles.org/PersonnelSelection.php for more information.

IGNITING MINISTRY GIFTS IN ALL CHRISTIANS

Section Five brings the book home. If the goal of Christian leadership is to help others fulfill God's will for their lives, the role of a leader is never done until every person they work with is on the road to becoming all God created them to be.

The picture of who we are ultimately is a picture of what life will be like in heaven. The task of Christians is to bring the reality of heaven into this world and let that reality become a powerful change agent in our world. "Your kingdom come, your will be done, on earth as it is in heaven" (Mt 6:10).

23

How God Loves Each
Person Differently

*Why else were individuals created, but that God, loving all infinitely,
should love each differently? . . . If all experienced God in the same
way and returned Him an identical worship, the song of the Church
triumphant would have no symphony, it would be like an orchestra
in which all the instruments played the same note. . . . Each has
something to tell all the others—fresh and ever fresh news of the "My
God" whom each finds in Him whom all praise as "Our God."*

C. S. Lewis

Wow! Think about that! The love God has for you is infinite: it
has no beginning or end; it is everlasting. Not only that, but
he loves each one of us differently. The love he bestows on you from
his limitless storehouse is unique, personal and meant exclusively for
you. That love is extended to every person from the heart of God. All
humans who answer to God's love with a responding love give back to
God and others an expression of love that only they can give. God's
unique love for each person shapes his or her particular expression of
love, which Lewis calls the "fresh and ever fresh news" of God.

We communicate love to others through our gifts, both natural and
spiritual. God intends us to offer these gifts to others so they will be
helped, encouraged, challenged and strengthened. God uses each believer to convey these gifts. God entrusts gifts to a specific believer in

order to deliver them to specific people at particular times and places, so that they may receive a distinct message from God and be affected as he intends. In a sense, you are God's special delivery person. Often the message is something that only you can convey. This concept is what the New Testament means when it speaks of gifts:

> We have different gifts, according to the grace given to each of us. If your gift is prophesying, then prophesy in accordance with your faith; if it is serving, then serve; if it is teaching, then teach; if it is to encourage, then give encouragement; if it is giving, then give generously; if it is to lead, do it diligently; if it is to show mercy, do it cheerfully. (Rom 12:6-8)
>
> There are different kinds of gifts, but the same Spirit distributes them. There are different kinds of service, but the same Lord. There are different kinds of working, but in all of them and in everyone it is the same God at work. Now to each one the manifestation of the Spirit is given for the common good. (1 Cor 12:4-7)

The problem is that most Christians do not understand these verses nor live as if they were true. According to G. K. Chesterton: "The human race, to which so many of my readers belong, has been playing at children's games from the beginning, and will probably do it till the end, which is a nuisance for the few people who grow up."[1] Part of growing up as a Christian is to put to use the unique gifts God has given you. The focus of this book is that God has gifted each Christian to be strong in spirituality, chemistry or strategy.

Natural gifts are the physical, intellectual and emotional gifts God has given to each person. Natural gifts are considered inherent to a person and have their origin in biological makeup and temperament. God uses natural gifts to enhance one's ability to minister in the name of Christ.

Spiritual gifts are God-given abilities, enablements or capacities divinely bestowed upon Christians. They are freely given by God. They cannot be earned or merited. Spiritual gifts are conveyed by the Holy Spirit through us to the intended recipient. They are meant to benefit others and give God glory, not to benefit us or give ourselves glory. Ultimately they are meant to build up the entire church. The purpose of spiritual gifts is to edify, instruct, exhort, encourage and comfort.

These spiritual gifts are the supernatural graces that individuals use to help fulfill the mission of the church. They are described in the New Testament, primarily in 1 Corinthians 12, Romans 12 and Ephesians 4. How do natural and spiritual gifts interact? The following passage from Exodus makes clear that God uses both natural and spiritual gifts as we minister to people.

> See, the LORD has chosen Bezalel son of Uri, the son of Hur, of the tribe of Judah, and he has filled him with the Spirit of God, with wisdom, with understanding, with knowledge and with all kinds of skills—to make artistic designs for work in gold, silver and bronze, to cut and set stones, to work in wood and to engage in all kinds of artistic crafts. And he has given both him and Oholiab son of Ahisamak, of the tribe of Dan, the ability to teach others. (Ex 35:30-34)

Both natural and spiritual gifts are expressed in the artistic craftsmanship of Bezalel and Oholiab. God also gave them the ability to teach and train others in this God-bestowed gift.

Different understandings of spiritual gifts have often created much controversy and division in the church. I will attempt to take the middle ground between cessationists (who say that some spiritual gifts are not for this age) and charismatics (who accentuate certain spiritual gifts) as I focus on how natural and spiritual gifts correlate with the six styles of leadership.

In table 23.1, I have listed all possible gifts and grant you, the reader, the option to customize it to your own theology. When only one leadership style is listed for a given gift, that style is the most predominant one that uses that gift. When two to five styles are listed, the order of listing indicates the sequence of their prominence. When you see "All styles," none is most prominent; the gift is present in all styles.

Table 23.1. Spiritual Gifts and Leadership Styles

Gift Cluster	Most Prominent Style(s)
Administration	Building leader
Apostleship	Mission leader
Craftsmanship	Sacred leader
Creative communication	Inspirational, imaginative, sacred and mission leaders
Discernment	Sacred, imaginative and mission leaders
Encouraging	Relational leaders
Evangelism	Inspirational, relational and building leaders
Faith	Mission, building, inspirational and imaginative leaders
Giving	All styles
Healing	Sacred, imaginative and relational leaders
Hospitality	Relational and inspirational leaders
Intercession	Sacred leaders
Interpretation	Imaginative and sacred leaders
Knowledge	Sacred, imaginative and mission leaders
Leadership	All styles
Miracles	Imaginative and sacred leaders
Pastor	Relational and sacred leaders
Prophecy	Imaginative and sacred leaders
Teaching	Sacred, imaginative and mission leaders
Tongues	Relational, sacred, imaginative and inspirational leaders
Serving	All styles
Showing mercy	Sacred and relational leaders
Wisdom	Mission and sacred leaders

God loves each person individually. He uses us to minister his touch through these unique gifts, to love and bless others in personal and specific ways. In return, God will use others to give back to us the blessing we need.

MISSION ASSIGNMENT — LEADERSHIP STYLES AND SPIRITUAL GIFTS

Look through the list in table 23.2 and consider which of the spiritual gifts in your column apply to you. The chart lists the most prevalent seven gifts of each style, arranged in alphabetical order.

Table 23.2. Most Common Gifts of Each Leadership Style

Sacred	Relational	Inspirational	Building	Mission	Imaginative
Craftsmanship	Encouraging	Creative Com	Administration	Apostleship	Creative Com
Discernment	Evangelism	Encouraging	Apostleship	Creative Com	Discernment
Intercession	Giving	Evangelism	Creative Com	Discernment	Faith
Knowledge	Faith	Faith	Encouraging	Faith	Knowledge
Mercy	Hospitality	Giving	Faith	Knowledge	Leadership
Pastor	Pastor	Hospitality	Giving	Leadership	Prophecy
Teaching	Serving	Leadership	Leadership	Teaching	Teaching

24

Working Together to
Serve and Love

*No work is insignificant. If a man is called to be a great sweeper, he
should sweep streets even as Michelangelo painted, or Beethoven
composed music, or Shakespeare wrote poetry. You should sweep
streets so well that all the host of heaven and earth will pause to say,
"Here lived a great street sweeper who did his job well."*

Martin Luther King Jr.

How can you help every member of your church or organization use his or her gifts? In what specific ways are your
people meant to serve?

I have had the opportunity to speak before many regional and national denominational meetings. These groups are typically made up
of more lay leaders than pastors. When I present the leadership stool
model to the group, I ask them to self-identify themselves as being
strongest in either spirituality, chemistry or strategy. I find that 95
percent of laypeople can accurately discern their strongest leg. I have
also noticed that laypeople are even more interested in this discovery
than are pastors. A simple place to begin is to help laypeople identify
their strongest leg. This will reveal the primary gift they bring.

If I may paraphrase Paul's words in Romans 12:6-8: If your gift is
spirituality, then use your spirituality gift in accordance with your
faith; if it is chemistry, then serve through your chemistry; if it is

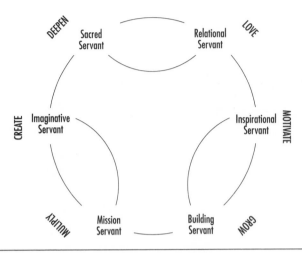

Figure 24.1. The six primary roles of Christian servants

strategy, then use your strategy gift to serve God.

For example, imagine you are asked to serve in the children's ministry of your church. If you are strongest in spirituality, teaching children or leading a ministry that prays for the neighborhood elementary school may bring you fulfillment and best utilize your gifts. If you are strongest in chemistry, your role may be to generate excitement and fun for the children as well as to create love and connection throughout the children's ministry. If you are strongest in strategy, your gift may be to organize the storage system, create a strategy to draw more children into the program or draw up a rotating teaching schedule. The same goes for any area of service. Whatever is your strongest leg, use that to serve God.

You can take members of your congregation to an even higher level of fruitfulness by helping them discover what style of servant they are and how they can best use that giftedness to serve God. There are six styles of Christian servants:

- ◆ sacred servants
- ◆ relational servants
- ◆ inspirational servants

- building servants

- mission servants

- imaginative servants

Each style expresses specific gifts that allow the ministry of your church or Christian organization to flourish.

✝ Sacred servants are designed to understand and experience the depths of the true God. They encourage spiritual depth through teaching the Bible, discipling Christians, explaining devotional practices and spiritual disciplines, and reminding Christians to look for and expect the work of the Holy Spirit. Sacred servants often use music, art, speaking, writing or craftsmanship to express their deep connection to God.

Relational servants are designed to spread love to the people around them. They create personal networks with and between people, both within and outside the church. They connect, engage, love and enfold. Relational servants are great at welcoming new people. They have an interest in getting to know individuals and quickly develop a genuine love for them. They inject joy in a group, bringing with them smiles and enthusiasm. Relational servants can transform a church or an organization into a united community.

Inspirational servants are designed to motivate teams and crowds of people to accomplish the mission of God in the world. They do this through a combination of excitement, energy, fun, focus and motivation. Inspirational servants create group enthusiasm. They often have the gift of an evangelist and are alert to people within their circle of friends who are not yet Christians.

Building servants are designed to create organized structures that allow the kingdom of God to have permanence and power in this world. Building servants are good at working with structures, plans, organization, management and administration. They excel at either expanding an organization or organizing and managing the details and structure of the organization.

↑ Mission servants envision the future and try to find new ways to expand and multiply the kingdom of God, especially outside the walls of the church. They are interested in finding opportunities from their neighborhood to the ends of the earth to assist and engage in living out God's mission. They may work with unreached people groups, assist in international community development, help launch new churches, or create structures of compassion, mercy and justice in economically challenged communities. They love to send out young leaders to multiply God's mission.

💡 Imaginative servants desire to use their creativity to connect the powerful gospel of Jesus Christ with their culture. Imaginative servants are not satisfied with the status quo and can help a church engage the emerging culture and at the same time prophetically speak against those who resist change and those who destroy God's good creation in people and in the world. They use fashion, innovation, imagination and creativity to stay on the cutting edge.

How do these six styles of servants work together to accomplish God's work in the world? 1 Corinthians 12:18-20 gives us a clue: "But in fact God has placed the parts in the body, every one of them, just as he wanted them to be. If they were all one part, where would the body be? As it is, there are many parts, but one body."

A STORY OF SERVANTS IN ACTION

My brother-in-law Brian and his wife, Pam, live in northwestern Minnesota. They worship at Trinity Lutheran Church, a 140-year-old country church in the tiny town of Holmes City. The main street consists of a general store, with an antique gas pump, and the church. In the summer of 2012, a friend of theirs, Dede Lemon, one of Trinity Church's members, asked the church council for permission to set up a vegetable stand in the corner of the church's parking lot on Saturday mornings. She wanted to sell the fresh produce that she raised in her large garden.

Dede is a relational servant whom everyone loves, so the council gladly agreed to her request. My sister-in-law Pam told Dede that she would keep her company. Pam would sell her homemade cinnamon rolls and coffee and give the proceeds to the church building fund. The small country churches all around Trinity were closing their doors, and Trinity's congregation was determined that they would not meet the same fate. By faith, they added a fellowship hall to their sanctuary, complete with a well-appointed kitchen and bathrooms, hoping to use it to do ministry that would attract locals to their fellowship.

Pam, an inspirational servant who tends to get excited about everything, was enthused about expanding their little farmer's market. She asked Dede if she knew of others who might be interested in joining with them on Saturday mornings. Dede was very well connected in the community, and soon there were seven vendors selling their goods at the Holmes City Farmers' Market. They didn't sell much that first summer, but they did have lots of fun together.

The market opened again the first week of June in 2013. Diane Kratz, a Trinity member and a building servant, had an idea. Since people were already coming to the farmers' market, why not invite them to breakfast? The church had been trying to develop a plan to reach out to their neighborhood, and offering breakfast might bring the neighborhood to them. On Friday evening, Diane and Pam set the tables in the fellowship hall and prepared the egg bakes they would serve the next morning. They had not asked for the church council's permission, fearing the members might not want their new carpet soiled.

Thirty people came to the first breakfast. Each person received a warm welcome, some delicious egg bake, a sausage and a cup of Dave Kratz's Swedish egg coffee. They had created a casual and comfortable environment where neighbors could meet neighbors, linger over coffee, get acquainted with each other and experience a sense of community.

My wife, Shelly, and I visited our brother- and sister-in-law the third weekend in July. They were excited about this new venture but said it was hard work. They were hoping that more people would come, and the offering barely covered their expenses. God prompted me to share Matthew 7:7 with them: "Ask and it will be given to you; seek and you will find; knock and the door will be opened to you." The mission leader in me encouraged Pam to ask, seek and knock—to pray and ask God to multiply their efforts. I could envision how God could use the breakfast and the farmers' market so that the pastor and the members of Trinity could build relationships with all those who gathered for breakfast. After driving home Saturday evening, Pam called the next afternoon to tell us that Pastor Denise had spoken on that very same verse in church that morning!

Word began to spread throughout the community about the breakfast and the farmers' market. The number of vendors grew to thirteen. Imaginative servants displayed their creative crafts—from wooden trivets and trinkets to beautiful, hand-sewn quilts. There were colorful flowers, berries, cheeses and freshly baked bread. The Jelly Man, dressed in suspenders and a straw hat, sold an amazing variety of delicious homemade jams and jellies.

The time had come for Pam and Diane to ask permission for what they had been doing for the past four weeks. How would the church council respond? The council exclaimed that this was one of the most exciting things that had happened to their church in all of its history. Not only was Trinity reaching out to its neighborhood by offering a place to build relationships and a sense of community, they were inviting them to become a part of Trinity's fellowship. Not only that, financially stressed families could enjoy a nutritious low-cost meal and buy fresh produce using food stamps. They were seeing new faces at the Sunday morning worship every week. Fifteen new people were now attending, including some of Dede's vendor friends, who filled an entire pew. All the proceeds from the breakfast's free-will offering were given to help pay off the new addition to the church.

On August 6, the local newspaper, the *Alexandria Echo*, published an article describing how Trinity Church was bringing "Unity to Their Community." On August 10, over one hundred people came for breakfast! They were becoming the hot place to be in Douglas County.

This story of Trinity Church demonstrates how each person plays an important role in carrying out the work of ministry. Dede, the relational servant, helped to begin the market by gaining approval from the church council and inviting her friends to participate as vendors. The vendors came and chose to stay because they like Dede. Pam, an inspirational servant, is very gifted at creating enthusiasm within a group. She makes sure to greet each vendor, visitor and church member and tells them how glad she is that they are there. She has a knack for creating an energetic and engaging atmosphere. She asks church members to contribute half an hour washing dishes and makes sure that they have a great time doing it! She tells stories, sings songs and makes them laugh. She also makes them feel their efforts are greatly appreciated.

Diane, the building servant, is the organizer. She takes care of the finances, advertises in the local paper, and procured a state grant for the farmers' market. She makes sure that all the details are covered each week. Denise, the pastor of the church, and Brian, my brother-in-law, are sacred leaders. They are there Saturday mornings to visit with people over breakfast, to get to know them, to love and care for them.

During the last week of August, a popular Minneapolis TV program planned to tape a segment on the closing of Holmes City's only business, the general store with its gas station. Diane contacted the TV station and was included in the segment. There she told the story of the Holmes City Farmers' Market and Trinity Church's breakfast. On the last Saturday in August, 220 people came to breakfast at Trinity Lutheran Church, and $760 was given in the free-will offering for the church's building fund!

No work is insignificant. If a person is called to be a relational servant, she should love people with all her heart, even as Michelangelo poured out his heart in his paintings. If a person is called to be an imaginative servant, he should create an expression of art even as Beethoven lovingly labored over his music. If a person is called to be an inspirational servant, she should inspire those around her even as Shakespeare still does through his poetry. And if you happen to be the person who sweeps the church parking lot after the farmers' market, you should sweep so well that all the host of heaven and earth will pass by and say, "Here lives the Holmes City parking lot sweeper, who does his job exceptionally well!"

SECTION FIVE ONLINE ACTIVITY: *A PASSION TO SERVE*— *A GIFT ASSESSMENT TOOL*

If the goal of Christian leadership is to help others fulfill God's will for their life, the role of a leader is never done until every person they work with is on the road to becoming all God created them to be. Yet most churches find that they have a difficult time getting even a minimal percentage of their members to know specifically how they are to serve God.

Beginning in the 1970s, spiritual gift inventories seemed to have much promise. Yet when churches tried to integrate this into actually mobilizing laypeople to serve in a specific role, it never seemed to work as well as it was advertised. The problem is that spiritual gift inventories are too complex, with up to twenty-three possible gifts to pick from. Even when people discover their spiritual gifts, then comes the task of helping everybody in the church find an appropriate place of service to use their gifts.

I have found that the simplicity of the leadership stool model makes it a more usable tool for laypeople—there are only three legs and six corresponding styles, making it easier to implement this model in a local church or a Christian organization.

"A Passion to Serve" is an online inventory that everyone in your church or organization can take. When individuals knows their strongest leg and their servant style, they become eager to serve. These motivated servants can then be connected to serve in a ministry where they already have gifts, aptitude and instinct. The result will be more ministry and more joyful servants. This program allows all your members to learn how God has created them to serve, and helps your church or organization know how to connect each person to a fulfilling place of ministry.

For complete information on "A Passion to Serve," please go to passiontoserve.com.

Appendix

Practical Advice for Implementing the Ideas of This Book

Celebrate your own gifts without downplaying your weaknesses. It is crucial to recognize, affirm and honor the gifts, passions and personality that God has given you. Most Christian leaders have too little clarity regarding their specific gifts, and receive too little encouragement in the use of them. Encouragement regarding the gifts God has given you is critical in releasing those gifts for ministry. But remember that self-awareness also includes recognizing your blind spots.

Make growth a daily priority. Your leadership strength will grow as you incorporate healthy habits of spirituality, chemistry, strategy and leadership wisdom into your daily life. It is not enough to want to be a leader or know what it means to be a leader. You need to have a commitment to grow as a leader and a specific plan and model to help you develop into who God wants you to become.

Seek to follow Jesus first. Christian leaders often take their cues from secular leadership principles—instead of understanding the radical nature of Christian leadership as articulated by Jesus. Study Jesus' model of leadership in the Scriptures and remember that your allegiance is to him first.

Employ your understanding of the styles in confirming your calling. You can use this model to understand in a deeper way your calling from God. This is discerned by recognizing your strongest leg, your natural and spiritual gifts, your passions, your personality and the fruit God produces through you—which is defined as human activity touched by the Spirit of God. Pray for, watch for and count the fruit.

Involve your family. If you're married, have you identified which is your spouse's leadership style? It can be the beginning of a fascinating conversation. You can also evaluate your children (or even your grandchildren) and determine what leadership style each of them possesses. Often you can determine this in children as young as three or four years old. It will give you insight into who they are, how they will function in life and how you can help them develop their best gifts.

Intentionally seek diversity. Surround yourself with a balanced group of friends and colleagues that reflect all six of the styles. It will give you great joy when you see God working through diversity. It will also enable you to see God's perspective from multiple points of view, reflective of the varied viewpoints different styles bring. If you discover that you are mainly spending time with people just like yourself, you will end up limiting your ministry fruitfulness through a lack of perspective. It is so enjoyable to watch how God uses different styles.

Invest time in leading young leaders. Very few Christian leaders do this intentionally. Form a group of three to four young leaders, and every other month participate in a specific activity together—give them an experience, don't just meet in your office! That will encourage deeper relationships and inspire fascinating conversations based on your shared experiences.

Get outside perspective. Having learned about the Leadership Stool model, you will quickly begin to understand some of the reasons why your church or Christian organization is ministering well. You will also discern the reasons why it has not been living up to some of its capabilities. Evaluate your Sunday morning service. Is it balanced with spirituality, chemistry and strategy? Ask a friend to visit your church sometime to look at it through fresh eyes. Ask them about their experience in each of these three areas. Do this with each of the ministries in your church or organization.

Visit other churches/organizations. It will help you to visit other church services or Christian organizations and write down and reflect on your first impressions. Did you feel welcome? Were you spiritually nourished? Were their purpose and momentum evident to you?

Incorporate other information to help determine a person's style. If you are not sure what style a person is, you can "reverse engineer" them by first attempting to discern which type of intelligence they possess, or their two deep needs, or the Ephesians 4:11 gift they have been given.

Refer to Ephesians 4:11. The Six Styles have a strong correlation with the gifts mentioned in Ephesians 4:11. Knowing this will give you better clarity on how you and others are to serve God.

Determine whether a team should be balanced or focused. Just as there are balanced leaders and focused leaders, there are also balanced teams and focused teams. Your primary leadership team should be balanced, making sure that spirituality, chemistry and strategy are equally represented. So should your primary ministry teams, such as children's, student, etc. All of these will benefit from multiple perspectives and varied gifts. Other teams function best when they are a focused team. Examples of this might be the prayer team, the financial team and other teams that have a specific focus.

Ensure that inspirational and building leaders are receiving spiritual nourishment. Inspirational leaders and building leaders are weakest in spirituality. That's not bad. God created them that way. God created them to be stronger in loving people and loving the mission of God. But this means that attention to their spiritual habits and accountability to others for their spiritual growth is critical.

Let God teach and humble you through experience. Many inexperienced leaders rate themselves higher than those with more experience and fruitful ministry. The more experience and fruit leaders have, the more God will show them how much more room they have to grow as they let God form and develop them.

Create common cause within your church/organization. The Leadership Stool model of leadership can help create a shared set of ideas that bind the group together, and a single coherent language through which to maintain common cause. Only when an organization has a shared set of ideas and a single coherent language will your church or organization see a "movement culture" develop.[1]

Notes

CHAPTER 1

[1]Winston Churchill (speech at the Royal Albert Hall on the creation of a united Europe, London, May 14, 1947).

CHAPTER 2

[1]Albert Mohler, *The Conviction to Lead: 25 Principles for Leadership That Matters* (Minneapolis: Bethany House, 2012).

[2]"50 Qualities of a Successful Leader from Mark Cuban, Daymand John, and Members of *Shark Tank*," *Brian Dodd on Leadership*, May 25, 2013, www.briandoddonleadership.com/2013/05/25/50-qualities-of-a-successful-leader-from-mark-cuban-daymond-john-and-members-of-shark-tank/.

[3]The Northumbria Community, *Celtic Daily Prayer* (New York: HarperOne, 2002), p. 17.

CHAPTER 3

[1]Martin Luther King Jr., "I've Been to the Mountaintop" (speech, Memphis, April 3, 1968).

[2]Henrietta Mears, *Dream Big: The Henrietta Mears Story*, ed. Earl Roe (Ventura, CA: Regal, 2012), p. 360.

[3]Quoted in Will Vaus, *Speaking of Jack: A C. S. Lewis Discussion Guide* (Hamden, CT: Winged Lion, 2011), p. 79.

[4]Tim Chester, "Lord of the Rings Pt 1: A Splintered Fragment of the True Light," *Tim Chester* (blog), October 2, 2010, www.timchester.wordpress.com/2010/10/02/lord-of-the-rings-pt-1-a-splintered-fragment-of-the-true-light/.

[5]Quoted in John Maxwell, ed., *The 21 Indispensable Qualities of a Leader: Becoming the Person That People Will Want to Follow* (Nashville: Thomas Nelson, 1999), p. 148.

[6]Max DePree, *Leadership Is an Art*, repr. (New York: Crown Business, 2004), p. 11.

CHAPTER 5

[1]Quoted in David Aitkin, ed., *Great Souls: Six Who Changed the Century* (Nashville: Thomas Nelson, 1998), p. 193.

CHAPTER 6

[1]Paul Caminiti (seminar, Santa Cruz, CA, May & September 2013).

[2]M. Robert Mulholland, *Shaped by the Word* (Nashville: Upper Room Books, 2000), p. 50.

[3]Ruth Haley Barton, *Sacred Rhythms: Arranging Our Lives for Spiritual Transformation* (Downers Grove, IL: InterVarsity Press, 2006), p. 111.

CHAPTER 7

[1]Rodney Stark, *The Rise of Christianity: How the Obscure, Marginal Jesus Movement Became the Dominant Religious Force in the Western World in a Few Centuries* (San Francisco: HarperSanFrancisco, 1997).

[2]Quoted in Donald T. Phillips, *Martin Luther King, Jr., on Leadership: Inspiration and Wisdom for Challenging Times* (New York: Business Plus, 2000), p. 58.

[3]Peter Lawler, "Religion and the Mind of the South," *First Things* (blog), August 2, 2013, www.firstthings.com/blogs/postmodernconservative /2013/08/02/religion-and-the-mind-of-the-south/.

[4]Donald T. Phillips, *Martin Luther King, Jr., on Leadership: Inspiration and Wisdom for Challenging Times* (New York: Warner Books, 1999), p. 153.

[5]Ruth Haley Barton, *Sacred Rhythms: Arranging Our Lives for Spiritual Transformation* (Downers Grove, IL: InterVarsity Press, 2006), p. 169.

CHAPTER 8

[1]David T. Olson, *The American Church in Crisis* (Grand Rapids: Zondervan, 2008), chapters 11-16.

[2]Donald Phillips, *Martin Luther King, Jr., on Leadership: Inspiration and Wisdom for Challenging Times* (New York: Warner Books, 1999), p. 330.

CHAPTER 9

[1]*Merriam-Webster's Collegiate Dictionary*, 11th ed., s.v. "instinct."

[2]Ibid.

CHAPTER 13

[1]Charles Spurgeon, "Elijah's Appeal to the Undecided" (sermon, May 31, 1857, Surrey, UK).

CHAPTER 15

[1]Tim Morey, *Embodying Our Faith: Becoming a Living, Sharing, Practicing Church* (Downers Grove, IL: InterVarsity Press, 2009).

CHAPTER 17

[1]Johannes Reimer (presentation, Evangelical Free Churches of Germany Conference, 2011).

CHAPTER 22

[1]Donald Phillips, *Martin Luther King, Jr., on Leadership: Inspiration and Wisdom for Challenging Times* (New York: Warner Books, 1999).

[2]Henrietta C. Mears, *Dream Big: The Henrietta Mears Story,* ed. Earl Roe (Ventura, CA: Gospel Light, 1990), p. 98.

[3]*Wikipedia*, s.v. "Eric Liddell," www.en.wikipedia.org/wiki/Eric_Liddell.

[4]Sally Magnuson, *The Flying Scotsman* (New York: Quartet, 1981), p. 143.

CHAPTER 23

[1]G. K. Chesterton, *The Napoleon of Notting Hill* (London: John Lane, 1904), p. 13.

APPENDIX

[1]Beverly Gage, "Why Is There No Liberal Ayn Rand?" *Slate*, August, 13, 2012, www.slate.com/articles/news_and_politics/history/2012/08/paul_ryan_and_ayn_rand_why_don_t_america_liberals_have_their_own_canon_of_writers_and_thinkers_.html.

IVP PRAXIS

EQUIPPING LEADERS FOR MINISTRY

"...TO EQUIP HIS PEOPLE FOR WORKS OF SERVICE,
SO THAT THE BODY OF CHRIST MAY BE BUILT UP."

EPHESIANS 4:12

God has called us to ministry. But it's not enough to have a vision for ministry if you don't have the practical skills for it. Nor is it enough to do the work of ministry if what you do is headed in the wrong direction. We need both vision *and* expertise for effective ministry. We need *praxis*.

Praxis puts theory into practice. It brings cutting-edge ministry expertise from visionary practitioners. You'll find sound biblical and theological foundations for ministry in the real world, with concrete examples for effective action and pastoral ministry. Praxis books are more than the "how to" – they're also the "why to." And because *being* is every bit as important as *doing*, Praxis attends to the inner life of the leader as well as the outer work of ministry. Feed your soul, and feed your ministry.

If you are called to ministry, you know you can't do it on your own. Let Praxis provide the companions you need to equip God's people for life in the kingdom.

www.ivpress.com/praxis